MW00775338

Liela,

Someone who knew both Oggy & Bob.

Best,
Jan Gifford

Always A Pleasure

JAN GIFFORD

RB
Remember-Books

ISBN: 978-0-9916209-0-6
ISBN-0991620909

TO FRIENDSHIPS

CONTENTS

INTRODUCTION

Friday Morning

Unfinished

What Would He Want Me to Do?

The File Folder

My Birthday Present

THE BEGINNING

Man in the Room

A Walk in the Neighborhood

Oggy, a Life Abridged

Poem: Heartache

Life Without Her

Studio 55

Hospitality

Poem: Falling in Love with Clay

My Studio?

Renaissance Men

Poem: Phone Calls

Healthy Living

Cupid

Bob Bowls

Office Supplies

Writing Biography

Poem: Everything I Needed to Know I Learned in

Writing Group

Serendipity

George

Reasons to Get Up in the Morning

Outside

Unexpected Gifts

Niko

Gravestone

Visiting Oggy

Poem: Oggy Silently Asks

The Call

Owls

Mortality

Sine Wave Vase

Wink

Sunny Days

Surprise Party

Friends to the End

Last Good-bye

Bermuda Green – A Letter to Bob

Poem: Night Light

Bob Light

Purple Bouncy Ball in the Sawdust

Blue Bunny

Poem: Empty Hangers

Tell Me – A Question to Bob

Scattering Ashes

Bereavement

ACKNOWLEDGEMENTS

Always A Pleasure

INTRODUCTION

Bob's wife Oggy, (her nickname for Olive since childhood) has Alzheimer's disease. Bob can no longer care for her at home. He is 78 years old and for the first time since their marriage 56 years ago, he is alone. His three children insist he "get out of the house."

I have been a potter for seven years at The Emerson Umbrella Center for the Arts when Bob enrolls in a pottery class consisting of seven women. I am 56 years old contemplating, with my husband Douglas, an empty nest as our fourth child, a high-school senior is applying to colleges.

Unpredictably, Bob and I become close friends for the rest of his life. The gender difference and the age difference make our friendship remarkable.

We take pottery classes at The Emerson Umbrella for the next 10 years. We set up a pottery studio at Bob's home, which we call "Studio 55" after Bob's house number on King Lane, where we spend hours at our side-by-side pottery wheels. In each other's company, everything we make receives attention and encouragement.

We eat lunch together and take afternoon walks in Bob's neighborhood. We enroll in additional pottery classes in nearby towns. We share serious conversation—"I don't think Oggy recognized me today," and dry humor—"It's such a lovely teapot but it leaks."

My husband Douglas and Bob become friends. MIT engineers, they share many common interests—pottery not among them; but kilns, yes!

Gentleman that he is, when I leave, Bob sees me to the door. I say some version of "good-bye." Bob says "Always a pleasure."

When Bob's son Brad introduces me to his friend at a family gathering, he says: "This is Jan. Dad and Jan do pottery together. Jan is Dad's... confidant, I think she knows him better than any of us."

This is our story. It begins at the end.

Apparently

there is

nothing

that cannot happen today!

Mark Twain

(1824 – 1921)

FRIDAY MORNING

Our bedside phone is ringing. We are still asleep. Who would call now, it's 7:45 AM?

I reach for the phone.

"Jan, it's Marcia. Dad died last night."

"No!" I say.

Isn't that what everyone says? "You didn't say what I think I heard."

But, of course, she did.

"But!" I say.

Isn't that what everyone says?

"But.... I was just there yesterday. We loaded the kiln. He was fine!"

"Oh no!"

Do the details matter? I suppose they help but change nothing. Apparently, Bob had a heart attack. His family was with him. Suddenly he is gone.

I hang up the phone and in my husband's arms cry inconsolably for two hours. Then I get up.

"I'm going over there," I say.

"Alone?" Douglas asks.

"Yes."

I let myself in with my key, into Bob's now empty home. The scent, (every home has one), greets me viscerally—warm and familiar. Bob's special lamp is still on—the lamp he made with the green pyramid shade. I numbly walk around our studio, my palm across my mouth, look at our clay-caked wheels. "We'll clean them tomorrow," we'd agreed yesterday. "Right now, let's have some tea," Bob said. No premonition could predict this. It is like a picture frozen in time. Only yesterday.....

Some motion catches my eye outside the plate glass door. Two little chickadees on the welcome mat, heads cocked, hopping back and forth. A blue jay perches on the eucalyptus, appears to be looking in the window. The chickadees don't fly away. I move closer to the door. They stay there, hopping closer.

"Are you looking for Bob?" I say right out loud. "He's not here," and I start to cry again.

Upstairs I see more birds outside Bob's windows—the pair of cardinals we know from lunches on the patio, goldfinches, nuthatches, and a tufted titmouse.

I decide they are a "sign." They have come to comfort me. Then, I notice, on the end table, the marble owl that matches mine. I pick it up and give it a sad little kiss, hold it in my pocket. I'll put them side-by-side.

UNFINISHED

Halloween was two days away. We were at our pottery wheels. "Are you ready for the trick-or-treaters?" Bob asked me. "Yes, Snickers and Milky Ways, what about you?"

"I think I'll make what I made last year."

I remember. He cut out jack-o-lanterns and glued on quarters for eyes. Bob's house is on a quiet lane, but a handful of neighborhood children come knocking. He would have been prepared.

In his office Bob's hand-designed note cards picturing ferns and gingko leaves, pine and winterberries are stacked beside the paper cutter ready for cutting and folding.

His computer is humming, awaiting the questions aimed at Google, the reliable resource Bob consults several times a day. On the table next to the printer is his frequently used digital camera. He took my picture yesterday afternoon.

In the living room on the table beside his chair are yesterday's completed crossword puzzle, the current issue of *Ceramics Monthly* and a library book.

Downstairs, his whites are in the washer, the darks in the laundry basket ready for the next load.

On Bob's pottery wheel, the bowl he just finished throwing yesterday is ready for trimming today. The kiln is loaded and the firing clicked off last night. It is still too hot for me to open. The graph where Bob faithfully recorded the rise in temperature inside the kiln is on his cluttered workbench.

This is Bob's unfinished life the day he dies, at the age of 89.

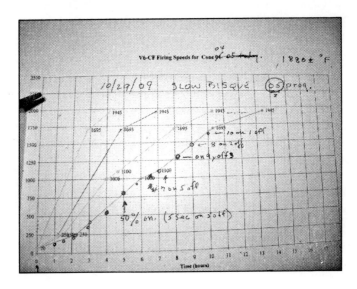

WHAT WOULD HE WANT ME TO DO?

I am alone in Bob's living room. This is not unusual. Frequently I am alone here. Bob will have left me a note. He may be back before I leave. He may be visiting Oggy or his sisters Doris or Maxine in Maine and be gone all day.

No! Not this time. This time he has not left me a note. He will not be back later. Bob will never be back.

I wander from the living room to the kitchen. Would Bob be surprised that I am crying at his kitchen counter in front of the coffee maker? Likely not. What would he want me to do?

Would he want me to water his plants—his ancient Christmas cactus or the flowering pink kalanchoe in the Bermuda Green flowerpot he made?

In the living room I sit in the chair he sat in yesterday, the day he died. We talked and had tea and cream cheese brownies before loading the kiln. What will happen to our studio—our wheels, our slab roller, his kiln, all our clay, and his pottery tools and books?

His notecards. Bob would want his notecards noticed. He spent hours perfecting size, intensity of color, placement, and design. He even printed RCButman Designs on the bottom of the latest ones. Like everything Bob did, his notecards were meticulous. When he printed one he was satisfied with, he labeled it a "master." His obvious intention was to make more.

I suggested selling them in packs of six at the gift shop where some of my pottery is sold.

"We can make a cover card with miniature images of the six designs," Bob proposed

In his office, the production is well under way. Card stock is piled here, finished notecards over there. I look for the ones with the red and orange maple leaf. Here they are. Bob had a plan, just not enough days before he died. Would he want me to cut the recently printed notecards and put them with the matching cream-colored envelopes?

I walk around the corner to his bedroom, stand beside his bed—the place he died last night. The shirt and pants he wore are laid beside his pillow—his turquoise shirt, his clay stained khaki pants.

On his green blanket lined up, as if with intention, are the contents of his pockets and his wristwatch, his favorite pen (a black deluxe micro mini ball) always in his left shirt pocket, his pocket change. But where is his wallet? Where is the half of a dollar bill he has carried around for eight years? I might not have remembered, but he showed it to me recently. It is a souvenir of a time we had tea at The Tea House in Wenham, Massachusetts. We squabbled about who should leave the tip.

"Let's split it," Bob said, and tore a dollar bill in half and handed me half and kept the other half, then saved it in his wallet all these years.

I'm smiling, now I'm crying. I don't know what he would want me to do.

THE FILE FOLDER

Bob's family gathered in his living room that afternoon. His daughter Marcia called me at home.

"Jan, we have something to give you if you'll stop by."

She knows I was there that morning. Alone, walking around the rooms, crying. Go back? What will they give me? —Bob's daughter Marcia, his sons John and Brad.

I stand on Bob's doorstep. Look at his pineapple doorbell. Do I just walk in? I tap the bell lightly, let myself in and stand at the bottom of the stairs—the stairs I have climbed hundreds of times for more than eight years.

"Please come up Jan," says Marcia, standing at the top of the stairs just like Bob often did.

They are all there talking in Bob's living room—Marcia and Toby, Nancy and John, Farley and Brad. I don't know what to expect.

"We found this in Dad's file cabinet, Jan. We haven't read anything. We think you should have it," Marcia says, handing me a bulging olive green hanging file folder.

"Jan" it reads on the glassine tab. Inside are pictures of me at my wheel, me outside sitting on a stool beside the front garden trimming a pot, a picture he showed me only days ago taken at Walden Pond last year, enlarged to 8x10. Every postcard. Every birthday card. Every little note I left on his pottery wheel. The poems I wrote and shared with him. Bob saved it all. I am speechless. I shake my head in disbelief, thankful the others are talking with one another, not observing my reaction.

Marcia hugs me. There are no words left.

MY BIRTHDAY PRESENT

Countless times Bob has surreptitiously left a plain brown bag containing a whole cored sweet juicy pineapple from Wilson Farm in a plastic container on the threshold of our side door. Starting with the first pineapple snack he served with tea the day we set up a studio together, we have had a "thing" about pineapple. Over the years as Bob continued serving and delivering pineapple I started finding pineapple gifts for him—a pineapple-shaped wooden bowl, a brass pineapple doorbell, pineapple magnets and coasters.

When I come home with the file folder I cannot bear to look through, my husband Douglas attempts to ease our heavy-hearted sadness with an excursion. My birthday is in five days and he wants to buy me something I have been wishing for—a granite mailbox post. He has done some research, and tucks me in the car for a mystery trip to a stone yard several miles away.

We talk of Bob, of course. Douglas drives. I cry.

I have admired and measured a granite post I like at a house in town. I know what I want—

rough-hewn grey granite, six inches square, all four sides rough with our house numbers engraved in black and a plain black mailbox.

At the stone yard, a young man named Mark takes us "out back."

"Here's what we have. This here with two sides smooth—that's called thermal finish, and this here with two sides rough—that's called rock face, or that one over there, not quite so rough, called Pineapple finish."

Pineapple? He said pineapple?

"Seriously, it's called pineapple?" I ask stupidly.

"Yes, Ma'am, that's right."

Is this additional unexpected consolation, like the birds looking in the studio window this morning? Pineapple granite? I like to think Bob might be smiling from afar knowing this will comfort us, lessen our sadness?

I look at my husband. He smiles knowingly and shrugs his shoulders.

"I think that's the one we want," he tells Mark.

"Happy Birthday."

THE BEGINNING

MAN IN THE ROOM

It is January, the start of the winter session of "Exploring Your Way with Clay," a Tuesday morning pottery class of seven women. Our instructor, also a woman is a professional potter. We have been together during the fall semester. The atmosphere is chatty. Talk of movies, restaurants, and our families and children. Life stories surface. We bond. We gossip. We relax at our wheels as the clay spins. Serendipitous therapy.

Enter Bob—a tall older gentleman, shock of snow-white hair, small mustache, turquoise flannel shirt with pocket protector, khaki pants, grey New Balance sneakers, pale rimmed eyeglasses and two hearing aids. Everything changes. There's a rooster in the hen house!

What brings him here? What's his story? We all wonder. When he is out of the room, we speculate.

At the next weekly class he tells me quietly, so as not to be overheard, his eyes fixed on the tabletop.

"My wife has Alzheimer's disease. I could no longer care for her. She is now in a care facility in Boston. My children suggested I take this class, so here I am."

He is subdued. For a man with double hearing aids he speaks in a very soft voice. I am careful not to "speak up" assuming he won't hear me. His story is heartbreaking, briefly told, and too painful for him to elaborate.

Looking up, he changes the subject. "I'm pretty much new at all of this, how about you?"

"This is my seventh year, I'm pretty much addicted, watch out!"

He smiles and I realize his two hearing aids work just fine.

"Remind me of your name," he says.

"It's Jan. If I can help, please ask."

Bob takes to the clay immediately. He buys his own tools. He keeps scrupulous notes in a green spiral notebook—date, dimensions of each piece, a simple sketch and the glazes he used. He is critical of his work. "Too heavy. Glaze not shiny enough. Throw it out. Try again." He is precise and persistent. He is an engineer.

Each potter is given a large shelf for storing supplies and clay. Bob's shelf is just above mine. His is meticulously tidy. Mine is tumbled together, piled high and crammed full. He shakes his head and smiles. I shrug. His turquoise flannel shirt has barely a splotch of clay on it. My kelly-green scrubs are clay-caked on sleeves and knees.

"Where did you get your.... outfit?" he says looking me over.

"Oh this, my jolly green giant suit? I think it's old hospital scrubs. I found it in a thrift shop in Vermont."

"Just the thing," he says with a wry smile.

I share my knowledge of studio glazes. He is appreciative. "Too many," he concludes, looking at the sample board of test tiles with overlapping colors—hundreds of them. "Looks like the sky's the limit. I think I'll stick with one or two."

Bob is a careful and calculating potter. I am a sloppy and playful potter. His first bowls are even and true. I called my first pots "soft serve"—wavy and a bit collapsed like a melting Dairy Queen cone.

Our class relaxes into storytelling again. Bob keeps to himself. Does he listen? His occasional comments reveal the answer. He is observant and quick-witted. We find out he has lived in town for nearly 50 years. He invents a tool for measuring the thickness of the clay at the bottom, then another to measure the thickness of the sides, then one to hold the bowl while dipping it into the five-gallon bucket of glaze. Wow! He's undeniably brilliant! Welcome Bob!

Our acquaintance becomes friendship when winter turns to spring and we walk around the block to the center of Concord for coffee. We live in a pedestrian-friendly town with ten crosswalks within an eighth-of-a-mile radius, coffee stops galore, and dog bowls of water at the base of the Library steps and on the sidewalks outside shops. It is May and shop doors are propped open letting in the lilac-scented breezes. Back at the Umbrella studio we enjoy our lunch outside at the sunny picnic table. We find we know people in common. We talk about our children—Bob's children are my age. My children are the ages of his grandchildren.

Bob glazes his bowls and vases a color called Bermuda Green, a shade of turquoise—the color of his flannel shirts—the color he glazes almost all his work—his favorite color—the color of his bedroom drapes. Wait! How do I know the color of Bob's bedroom drapes? Wait.

Methinks

that

the moment

my legs begin to move

my thoughts

begin to flow."

Henry David Thoreau

(1817-1862)

A WALK IN THE NEIGHBORHOOD

Probably the turning point in our friendship comes the spring day I ride my bike to Bob's house and ring his doorbell.

Bob lives in a contemporary house—big windows everywhere. Even in his ground floor entrance level—the glass door and the wall of windows let the sunshine stream into the south facing room.

He is shocked to see me on his doorstep.

"Why hello JAN!"

"Would you like to go for a walk?" I ask.

"Are you serious?"

"Of course, it's such a nice day and you told me you like to take a daily walk."

"Why yes I do. Won't you come in? I'll get my jacket."

"I ordinarily take about a mile and a half trek around the neighborhood. Are you up for that?"

"Sure, that's fine."

We set off.

"Where is your car?" He asks as we approach his empty driveway.

"Oh, I rode my bike."

Looking incredulous, Bob leads the way.

Neighbors wave hello. (Who's that with Bob?)

"I am so fortunate to live in such a friendly neighborhood. We all settled here about the same time in the 50's when this part of town was just getting developed. Many of us are still here 50 years later. Our house was the model home to advertise building a home here. It was outfitted with rented furniture and there was a fountain in the corner of the living room, if you can imagine!"

I later discover Bob is on the Board of Directors of the association of 100 contemporary-style homes similar to his. Also, that he wrote "The Conantum Saga"—a colorful history, including pictures, of the development of that area of Concord. had it printed, spiral bound, and made it available to everyone. There is a copy of it in the Local History section of the Concord Library.

"Have you time for a cup of tea?" he asks as we complete the circuit.

OGGY, A LIFE ABRIDGED

I can't describe Bob as a happy man. His wife of over 50 years is not going to get well. His devotion to her is extraordinary. He visits her every day. She responds to him with a bewildered smile.

Bob makes picture books for Oggy on colored construction paper—pasted on magazine pictures with words under the pictures. "Pears," "Grapes." "Happy," written under a big picture of a person smiling.

He plants a row of flowers along the south side of the nursing home where he takes Oggy for a wheelchair stroll in the sunshine. He tends a greenhouse, hoping to engage the residents but that is impossible. Oggy needs a walker and requires help with dressing. I cannot imagine the agony of seeing the one you love more than anyone forgetting everything you have shared, eventually forgetting you.

Bob shows me photographs—Oggy on their boat. Oggy ice-skating on The Concord River. Oggy with their three children—Marcia, John and Brad. Oggy as his bride standing beside him—her groom at age 22—tall, dark, and handsome; Oggy, the daughter of the Mayor of Medford, a

Wellesley College graduate with a Masters' degree from Tufts, a guidance counselor, a member of the Concord School Committee, an experienced sailor, swimmer, skier and skater.

Several years before Oggy showed signs of Alzheimer's disease she watched as the debilitating disease claimed her older sister, June. When Oggy's forgetfulness progressed from misplacing her keys to forgetting the names of their children, her fear became a terrifying reality, and frustration and anger became depression. Bob's care for her was his sole activity—his responsibility entirely. Of course, their children shared the vigil. Two of the three, Marcia and John, live nearby, Brad, on Cape Cod, called his father every day. They said that it was too much for their Dad. Their mother should be in custodial care. Bob resisted.

A common story, yes, but until it is a personal reality, it is always someone else's story. One day Oggy "escapes." wandering in the yard, walking down the road, touching the mailboxes. Colleen, a neighbor, brings Oggy home. Had Bob turned his back, stepped into the house while Oggy was outside? No matter. No harm done, "Thank you Colleen;" but when it happens again and their children find out, arrangements are made and Oggy leaves their home on King Lane forever.

Painfully resigned, Bob drives their silver Volkswagen with Oggy beside him. In the back is the suitcase he packed with her clothes, her hairbrush and face cream, her slippers and robe, a coat (she would need a coat, wouldn't she?) to the first of three nursing homes where, for the next ten years Oggy will live a life in agonizingly slow decline.

Bob pushes her in her wheelchair and sings to her. He tells me: "If I put my hands on Oggy's shoulders, she shrugs and tilts her head to rest her face against my hand, and I could weep." She moves her head in time to the rhythm of Bob's singing, amazing him because, though eventually Oggy cannot speak and her eyes are puzzled or vacant, the songs he sings to her, "Swanee River," "Let Me Call You Sweetheart" and "You Are My Sunshine," seem to reach some still viable part of her damaged brain. This tender encouragement reinforces Bob's commitment made nearly 60 years ago—"for better or worse, in sickness and in health, as long as we both shall live."

Photo courtesy of Butman family

HEARTACHE

What does it taste like?
The cocktail of sadness
With a twist of relief?

You must hardly
Taste the twist
At first
Sip again.

You are accustomed to
Straight-up sadness
Sleeplessness and worry
What now?

Your worth was measured
Ounce by ounce
Getting through the day
Safely
All of it
Your responsibility.

Your best was not enough
Although you understood
It was inevitable
Surrender felt so tinged
With harsh reality.

Who will do what you have done?
Who will comfort and try to understand
All her pleading eyes convey?

Who will bathe and dress her now?
Fix her meals?
Help her with a fork
Or spoon?

You spent yourself
To the last drop.

Relinquishing that role
Is drenched in sadness.

You hope it wasn't all in vain.

LIFE WITHOUT HER

Insomnia. Nightmares. High blood pressure. Heartbreak is costly. Bob sees his doctor who prescribes blood pressure medication and pills for anxiety. His daily visits with Oggy and his chores and errands take up half his day. His son Brad calls every evening. His daughter Marcia is often there when he visits Oggy. His son John, and John's wife Nancy invite him to Sunday dinner. Bob treasures these visits, says they have lively conversation with his grandsons Henry and Jeremy.

"I have a wonderful family," he tells me. Neighbors visit. Newsletters remind him of Conantum meetings and events. *The Concord Journal* and *The Boston Globe* get a thorough perusal. The daily crossword is completed. Photography and printing photos are a continued interest. Bob takes a daily walk and gets 20 minutes of sunshine when the weather is fair. He has many friends whom he visits and helps with home projects from setting up and understanding their computers to repairing their broken garage doors. From his beach plum bushes he continues his yearly tradition of making jelly, which he gives to family and friends. Life without Oggy at home is surprisingly busy. And now there is Pottery!

"A friend is

a gift

you give

yourself."

Robert Louis Stevenson

(1850-1894)

STUDIO 55

In addition to the three-hour class time, potters may come to the Umbrella studio and work independently during the week. Bob's schedule and mine seem to synchronize and we are often there at the same time. Bob decides to buy a wheel and set up a home studio. I am likewise planning to build a home studio. Mine will involve groundbreaking and adding a room to our home, construction to begin soon. I have a pottery wheel that I am sharing at The Emerson Umbrella until my studio is complete. Bob's studio will be a conversion of his first level.

We compare plans.

Bob purchases a pottery wheel and is ready to convert his sunny ground floor room to a studio.

"I have some ideas but perhaps you would take a look and see what you think."

His large ground-floor room has a brick wall with an open wood-burning fireplace, orange shag carpet, two comfortable chairs, a gigantic 50-year-old Christmas cactus and many framed family pictures on the wall.

"What do you have in mind?

"Getting rid of the rug but there is ugly linoleum under it. I thought I could cover it with vinyl."

Bob chooses white vinyl with an aqua pattern. In his workshop full of carpentry tools and a large table saw he builds shelves for his pottery supplies and for setting drying pottery before and after trimming. He invites me to see the quickly finished room.

"Wow! What a transformation!" It's beautiful.

Bob even made wooden "coasters" to put under the feet of his new pottery wheel so it doesn't dent the vinyl.

"Why don't you bring your wheel here until your studio is ready? There's plenty of room for two."

I agree, and even before my husband helps me carry my wheel from Bob's driveway to the house, Bob has built a set of shelves like his, for me. He buys a radio/CD player, two space heaters in case it's chilly and a halogen floor lamp. We create a clay studio. We call it Studio 55—Bob's house number on King Lane—a speedy transformation to a sparkly white vinyl-floored fully equipped pottery studio, Voilà!

"Every day I visit my wife at the nursing home. I want you to be able come and go whenever you like. If I'm not home, feel free. I'll leave you a note. Here's a house key."

In my basement I find an old picture frame, and with letters and numerals from a craft store, a sheet of black poster board and a can of gold spray paint I create a Studio 55 sign to hang on the brick wall over the studio fireplace.

So begins our unique relationship. Bob's home becomes my home away from home. The studio is busy and messy—my side anyway. We leave work in progress, which necessitates return. With clay, it is all about timing, not too dry for trimming—covered and uncovered carefully so it doesn't dry too fast and crack.

I call to see if Bob is home.

"Hello, is this Studio 55? I would like to make a reservation."

And Bob answers: "Please hold, I'll have to check the book."

At least he didn't say. "Please listen carefully as our menu options have changed. Your call is very important to us and will be answered in the order it was received."

"Why, it appears we have an opening between 3:00 and 4:00."

I laugh. "And Bob, could you please uncover the three bowls I made yesterday. I'd like to come this afternoon to trim them."

"Yes I could, and yes, I shall," he says reminding me, as my father does, of the proper use of "could" and "would" and "can" and "may," and their correct meaning and frequent misuse.

Our wheels are side-by-side, shelves to our left, the radio and the floor lamp between us.

We talk. We don't talk. A CD called "Relaxing Piano Music" plays softly. Spinning, spinning, wet and smooth, our hands in clay. Pottery is a messy art. Wet clay gets on our clothes, the floor, sometimes on the walls. We lose track of time in that sense of flow that happens when totally absorbed in something you love doing.

"Will you have some tea?" asks Bob, breaking the silence.

"Yes, thank you, but I don't want to stop. Can, I mean, *may* we have tea at the wheel?"

"Of course."

Upstairs in the kitchen Bob is busy. I hear the whistle of a teakettle. Carefully he comes down the steep carpeted stairs carrying a tray. Tea in two turquoise cups he has made, a small pitcher of milk, two dinner sized paper napkins and a surprise snack—pineapple served in turquoise bowls each topped with a strawberry. "Wow, look at this. Elegant! Pineapple is my favorite!"

After that, now and again a juicy cored pineapple from Wilson Farm would appear in a brown bag on our doorstep. No note.

I jokingly call him my Pineapple King. He likes the title and the pineapple keeps coming. Pineapple in Studio 55 if we are there together and it's "time for tea."

For Christmas I give him a brass pineapple doorbell. Bob's doorbell has a shrill ring like a tricycle bell. If I peek in the glass door and he is not at his wheel, just a tiny tap gives a quick ding letting him know I am downstairs opening the unlocked door.

Pineapple—the symbol of hospitality.

HOSPITALITY

I tap the doorbell lightly and call "Hello" as I let myself in. Bob appears smiling at the top of the carpeted stairs to his living room area.

"Welcome JAN! Will you come up and sit for a bit?"

Sunshine suffuses his window-walled living room.

"Please be seated, I'll make us some tea."

We sit and talk, Bob in his clay clothes—turquoise flannel shirt out at the elbows, frayed collar, clay-spotted khakis, grey wool socks, and New Balance grey sneakers. I sit on the couch opposite "his chair." He leans back, relaxed man pose—his long legs outstretched. He rakes his fingers through his snow-white hair.

"So tell me a story."

I tell him about our youngest son Tyler's college search.

"It may be Cornell."

"My grandson is at Cornell doing graduate work," Bob responds, "good choice."

"Next year, empty nest for Douglas and me," I say, momentarily forgetting how empty Bob's nest is.

"What about you?" I say. "Looks like you've already been at your wheel today."

"Yes, I have a new idea for a triangular lamp base. I'll show you."

"Excellent, but first can I use the bathroom?"

"You can, and yes, you may."

"Oh, there I go again. I may and I shall."

Another touch of hospitality—every day Bob hangs a fresh fingertip towel in the bathroom just for me. When I return from a three-day weekend in Vermont I find three fingertip towels hanging there on Tuesday instead of one. He says if I go away for three weeks he will hang 21. Humor is essential. Dry humor is my favorite, and where does he get all these fingertip towels?

Bob is a soft-spoken man of few words, but quick and savvy. He truly listens and his responses are thoughtful.

"I love that you "get it," I tell him.

"We are on a wavelength," he says. He calls us "Particle 1 and Particle 2." It must be physics!

We lament about what Bob calls "the tedious task of shoveling the endless paper pile."

"Mine," I tell him, "piles up between the phone and the kitchen sink. When it cascades into the sink I know it's time to deal.'"

He laughs and says. "People tend to do what they want to do. We must want to talk, drink tea, and make pots."

"Yes, all of it. I wrote a poem after my first clay classes at The Emerson Umbrella—how I fell in love with the whole clay experience? When my teacher, Randy Huckins, read it he said he knew I was hooked and would be involved with clay forever."

"I would be interested in what you wrote."

"I'll find it and bring you a copy."

"I shall look forward to that."

"Meanwhile let's go make some masterpieces in our studio?"

"Indeed! Shall I make a fire in the fireplace today?"

My first pot

FALLING IN LOVE WITH CLAY

The spinning wheel
Mesmerizes me
I play with the clay
Wet and cool
Slipping through my fingers
Taking shape
Of what?

A new vocabulary
Slowly learned
"Wedge" and "Throw" and "Pot"
Mean something they didn't mean last week
And artists with experience
Tell me
The clay has "Memory."

"Rib," "Pin Tool," "Wooden knife"
With very little patience
I expect a masterpiece
Therefore everything I make
I see that way
I save it all.

My overalls are caked with clay
I get it in my hair
And on my face
I enjoy the mess
It makes me laugh

I have no sense of time
I mold the clay

In trance-like mood
Feeling
Seeing with my fingers
The thickness
And the form

In class
The instructor
Is talking to the clay
Or is he listening?
He says the clay will let him know
What it is meaning
To become

He takes our class
To the Museum of Fine Arts
To look at pots
From many cultures
Centuries past
Some very old
Some new

"Find one you like" he says
"Sketch it
Look Hard
Get it in your mind
Then you can make one similar"
And he is right

I found out only yesterday
That other people
Don't see spinning wheels
Before they fall asleep at night
I always do
If I have worked with clay
That day

And when I trim the bottom of a pot
Where I constantly watch
The turning clay
When I look away
The whole room seems to spin
In the opposite direction of the wheel
I figured this phenomenon
Was true for everyone

The glazes
Are another art to learn
With names I've never heard before
And can't remember or pronounce
Ohatakhaki, Temouku, Celadon
With apprehension
I dip my treasures

The firing of the kiln
Is magic

From the still warm kiln
Our teacher lifts
Each shining pot
Holding one-by-one
In a spotlight
Commenting on its beauty

I hold my first glazed pot
Warm in my hands
Smooth and heavy
Bent and uneven
I am thrilled
Did I make this
With just a lump of clay?

Jan Gifford, February 1991

MY STUDIO?

Bob is turning 80. Let's have a party! Lunch at my house with the studio potters—Selena, Marjorie, Carol, Amy, Karen, and Bob's daughter Marcia. Each of the potters gives Bob something she has made. He appears uncomfortable with the attention but quietly pleased. He brings me a hostess gift—a bouquet of pussy willows and a garden trowel.

"The trowel is for your groundbreaking. I hope it doesn't go too fast."

Implied of course, is that once my studio is complete I will move my wheel from his house to mine.

Bob's hope becomes reality. Progress is slow. Reluctance to make the transition to my newly constructed studio is understandable. Although eventually vinyl flooring is installed, the paint color is chosen, and the elaborate lighting is completed, there is no word of "the move." My wheel remains at Studio 55.

Bob and I are happier working together than either of us would be alone. There is no schedule. His visits with Oggy are random. His note on my wheel: "Be back around 1:00." He does errands, keeps appointments, and visits friends. With my key I come and go whenever I choose.

RENAISSANCE MEN

I know they will have a million things in common. It's time my husband Douglas and Bob become friends.

Although they are both MIT-educated engineers their interests and eclectic knowledge make them Renaissance men.

Sailing, for instance. Douglas sails small boats. Bob sailed larger boats—boats they could sleep on. They share stories from sailing adventures and, even more interesting, memorable misadventures.

They are gardeners. Douglas grows vegetables. Bob plants tomato and pepper plants at Oggy's nursing home, herbs on his patio and flowers out front.

We sit in Bob's living room, three instead of two. Conversation progresses from sailboat lingo to gardening, to WWII submarines, to telescopes, to Quantum mechanics, to quarks. Quarks? I leave the room. I don't think they even notice.

Bob's 33-year old clothes dryer suddenly quits. High time for a new one? Oh no! Together they pull it out, take off the back, do some measurements with Bob's voltmeter, get some serial number somewhere, order parts online and fix it. "Good as new," they proclaim, "they don't make them like this anymore!"

They read books with scholarly titles: *Quantum Evolution, Descent into Chaos, The Origin of the Cosmos,* and *Flow* and they understand and discuss them! I read Maya Angelou's autobiography.

We decide to buy a kiln, actually two—one for our garage, one for Bob.

Because Bob's will be inside the house, it requires special installation and ventilation. Just the project for Bob and Douglas! Together they design a venting system using half a barbecue grill, some dryer hose, a window fan, a timer and a pyrometer. They discuss wavelengths, ohms and resistance, calibrations and rates of climb—this to do with the gradual heating of the kiln. Bob makes graphs and using a pyrometer placed into the side of the kiln to measure the temperature, he records the specifics of the firing every hour when his kitchen timer dings.

Bob needs a better handrail leading from upstairs to our studio. At Concord Lumber, he buys the railing, stains and varnishes it and together he and Douglas install it.

They become basement buddies, admiring each other's skills and tinkering with tools. They are living room intellectuals appreciating each other's knowledge and intelligence, discussing "highbrow stuff." They are Renaissance men. They are friends.

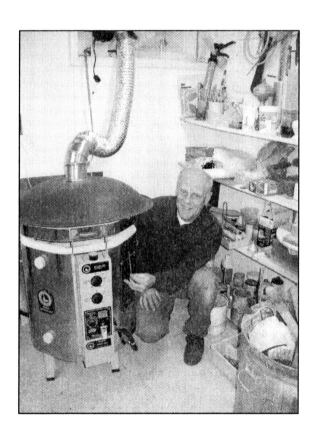

JAN GIFFORD

PHONE CALLS

Bob, by example
Teaches me something profound
When I call him on the phone and say
"Hi, it's Jan."
Every time he says
"Hello JAN!"

We often sit
In his sunny living room
Having tea and talking
The phone rings
And of course he says
"Hello."
Then "Hello MARCIA!"

He's so glad to hear your voice
He uses your name
With enthusiasm

And
After our conversation
Right before he says
"Good-bye."
He always says
"Thank you for checking in."

This courtesy
Bob taught me inadvertently
Using the caller's name
Now comes naturally to me

"Father Time

is not always a hard parent,

and, though

he tarries

for none of his children,

often lays his hand lightly

upon those

who have used him well"

Charles Dickens

(1812-1870)

JAN GIFFORD

HEALTHY LIVING

Bob is vigilant. Realizing the cost of the alternative, his diet and exercise regimen are high priorities.

Before it becomes all the rage, Bob's diet is low fat—not a stick of butter in his fridge, and no salt—he doesn't even *have* a saltshaker. No mayo on his lean turkey sandwich, freshly squeezed lemon juice on his salad, no hollandaise sauce on his broccoli. Vegetables from Wilson Farm, fish three times a week. No red meat. No mashed potatoes and gravy. Fruit for dessert.

Also no sugar. In Studio 55 Bob makes a lovely sugar and creamer set. The sugar bowl remains empty and so does the creamer. He drinks his tea and coffee without either. I introduce him to cream cheese brownies but they are not the obsession they become for me. He will eat one, not six.

He walks in his neighborhood—over a mile every day. He lifts blue eight-pound dumbbells that he keeps beside his living room chair. Bicep curls, overhead presses, side bends, forward rolls.

According to *Yoga Journal*, "You are as young as your spine is flexible."

"After Fifty It's A Matter of Maintenance," reads a framed poster on my friend's kitchen wall. Show me a person over 60, never mind 80, without a few, if not an arsenal of medications for hypertension, high cholesterol, back pain, thyroid disorder, sleep apnea, or arthritis. Bob is conscientious but not exempt.

He manages his hearing loss with very expensive hearing aids. For hypertension he takes medication. He keeps a blood pressure log in his black spiral-bound notebook, which he entitles "Body Data." For his atrial fibrillation, he does dogged research. On his computer he composes copious notes for his doctors, and he "frets."

"This seems to be the one thing I can't get quite right," he groans.

Bob makes the very best of what he is given. He is given 89 excellent years.

CUPID

Under different circumstances I think they could have made the perfect couple—my good friend Ruth and Bob. But this idea of mine has many things working against it—Bob's life-long commitment to Oggy, and Ruth and Bob's homes being 100 miles apart.

I might never have thought of their compatibility until one day when Bob tells me he will be missing our Tuesday morning pottery class at The Umbrella because he is going to Kennebunk, Maine to visit his sister Doris who is in a nursing home.

"I have a friend Ruth who lives in Kennebunk. Next time you go, maybe we can go together. You can visit Doris. I can visit Ruth. I'll drive."

"That sounds like a interesting idea," says Bob, skepticism barely concealed in his look of surprise

"I would love to introduce you to my friend Ruth. You'll love her. She's just like you!"

Now Bob looks really worried. Where is this woman coming from? his furrowed white brows convey.

But I go on.

"Ruth is more intelligent and well-read than anyone I know. She has a 40-year career as an indexer of books—mainly for Little Brown, Inc. Imagine having to read a book you know nothing about, then figure how to write the index? Ruth is a marvel—soft spoken and whip smart—just like you!"

Bob is speechless. I let it be.

About a month later after our Tuesday morning pottery class Bob says hesitatingly,

"Were you serious about a trip to Maine together?"

"Sure, do you have a time in mind?"

"It's up to you. Doris isn't going anywhere, it's safe to say."

"No, sadly I suppose she isn't. I will talk with Ruth."

Ruth listens. A further coincidence is that Ruth's good friend lives at the same nursing home as Bob's sister Doris. Everyone can visit everyone!

I remember our first trip to Maine. As I drive along Route 495 Bob pulls an index card from his shirt pocket.

"I've prepared a list of topics of conversation for our car ride."

I am astonished and smiling. What a practical idea. Consider the challenge: What does a politically savvy intellectual engineer discuss with a woman he knows from his pottery class? For an hour-and-a-half drive each way!

It turns out to be family stories. We don't listen to the radio. A lull in conversation does not feel awkward. We just talk. Bob is an attentive listener and he tells a good story. I especially like the one about his sister Maxine. "Maxine the Beauty Queen," he calls her. (She truly was a beauty queen years ago), but now "she does absolutely nothing all day. Her boyfriend Bill waits on her hand and foot which is what she expects and what she gets. Their house is like a giant knick-knack museum. It drives me crazy going there and seeing how they just sit around all day."

"Seems you and Maxine have very little in common. It's so kind, Bob, that you visit both your sisters."

"I'm the baby. Doris is 12 years older and Maxine is eight. I think I was probably a mistake."

A good mistake, if so.

Bob and Ruth are cordial and at ease. We have lunch at a casual restaurant overlooking the water. Bob asks Ruth about her Indexing and is duly impressed with the seemingly impossible task and the titles she has recently indexed. Ruth directs us to a local pottery studio in Kennebunk in an out-of-the-way spot. We admire the pottery and gather ideas for work in our studio at home.

On our car ride back to Concord I realize Bob expected Ruth to be my age, not his.

"Tell me how you and Ruth came to know each other."

"I have known Ruth for over 30 years. We met when our daughter Jennifer was just a baby and I was walking to the library pushing the baby carriage up the hill. Ruth and her husband Grosvenor lived on the corner across from the library. They had a golden retriever named Nicholas who walked to the village store with them and, like something you might expect in a

Norman Rockwell painting, carried the mail home in his mouth.

They owned a blue 1959 Mercedes 300d. I knew Douglas would admire it and we stopped to chat. Later Douglas and Grosvenor became fast friends. He and Ruth became like family. Grosvenor was an inventor type, liked gadgets, figuring out new ways to fix something—just like my husband, like you Bob. You would have enjoyed him. He ended up selling Douglas the Mercedes for $500.

"And Grosvenor?"

"He died several years ago. He was 23 years older than Ruth."

To my delight, Bob and Ruth thoroughly enjoy each other's company. After she moves from Maine to Brattleboro, Vermont we invite them for a weekend to our vacation home. Bob drives to Brattleboro, picks up Ruth and meets Douglas and me at Hildene, the Lincoln family estate in Manchester Vermont. We then go to our Vermont vacation home for the weekend. We swim in the lake, Bob and Douglas have a sail in our Laser sailboat, and we go to a farmer's market, and a Sunday evening band concert on the Town Green.

I can still picture them sitting in our backyard having a glass of wine on a summer evening while I prepare dinner. It is a mutual friendship with only the miles between them in the way.

BOB BOWLS

"Try throwing with your eyes closed," I suggest, seated at my wheel beside Bob's.

"What? Why would I do that?"

"Because by now you don't need to look. You could throw a perfect porcelain bowl in your sleep."

"Is that what you do?" he says as he looks to see the cylinder I have been trying to raise to ten inches slowly collapse in my cupped hands.

We laugh and Bob returns to his systematic, measured, engineer's approach to perfection using his ruler, compass and his recent invention requiring a suspended string to measure the exact diameter of his bowl.

Bob's bowls are recognizable on a shelf among the work of a dozen potters. There is symmetry between the height of the bowl, its width at the rim and the dimension of the foot (the base). Whether it is a small bowl (which he calls "handy little bowls"), or a cereal or fruit bowl, Bob's bowls are proportionally designed. I wonder if this calculated intent is inevitable with his engineer's mind.

My bowls, on the other hand, are swoopy and scalloped and altered with a cheese slicer, something to which Bob would never submit his pots.

"There is no right or wrong in art," Bob says, ever so kindly. "You make five bowls while I make one."

"Yes, and yours survive to contain salad and mine are hysterical experiments that end up in the recycle pail."

"And we are having fun!" he says. "You told me it's just 'playing with the clay.' Indisputable, I couldn't agree more!"

OFFICE SUPPLIES

Google was "born" in 1998. It is Bob who introduces me to this phenomenon over a year later.

"Looking for a white stoneware clay? We can ask Google."

Google? I don't know what he's talking about, which today seems inconceivable because we feel that Google has always "been there."

"Ask Google absolutely anything you want to know about, and Bingo! There you go! Come into my office and I'll show you."

Down the hall from Bob's sunny living room is his office. A cushy gray tweed swivel chair rolls in front of the large monitor of his desktop computer.

"Please, sit down, I'll demonstrate."

Of course now Google is a household word, if not a necessity. However, at the turn of the century, Bob at age 80 is on the cutting edge of technology, using it daily. An inveterate researcher, he shows me how he searched, compared features and read online reviews before he ordered his 100 pound pottery wheel delivered to his door—free shipping. Wow!

Within 15 minutes, Bob has converted me to a Google addict too. And that's not all!

We discover we share a love of photography, and with Bob's high-quality color printer and glossy photo paper, he shows me how he crops and enlarges and prints photos of family, friends, and flowers.

"This printer is a lot of fun. Watch this!"

He selects a color snapshot of his daughter Marcia as an adorable little four-year-old and sets it in the copier. He selects an 8 ½ x 11 sheet of glossy photo paper from his stack on the shelf, pushes a couple of buttons, scrolls through a menu, clicks on a selection and pushes "Print." Rumble rumble, out pops an 8x10 enlargement, not in color but in sepia, looking like an antique portrait.

"Well, well, Mr. Butman, I am duly impressed."

"Feel free to use this anytime you like. I'll teach you, there's nothing to it."

On Bob's worktable are his office supplies. I have favorites. I love his paper cutter. They don't make them like this anymore—heavy wooden base, mighty blade, chop chop!

"I want this paper cutter!" I tell him.

"It's a good thing I have this paper cutter. Do you come to see me, or is it my paper cutter?"

"No," I tell him, laughing, "It's your printer. I can't print photos at home."

He laughs too, but the very next day he buys me deluxe high gloss photo paper in two sizes—4x6 and 8x10. "Use it up, now that you know how."

Among my favorites are Bob's gold paper clips. "Such a luxury compared to the common ones," I tell him

Months later, for my birthday Bob buys me a box of my very own gold paper clips and, to make a point, he also gives me three five-inch-long brass paper clips with this note:

"To hold your life together,

Love, Bob."

When Marcia and her brothers begin to dismantle Bob's home she says,

"Jan, please take anything you want from Dad's office. We don't need any of it."

So now Bob's coveted paper cutter and his fancy printer are mine.

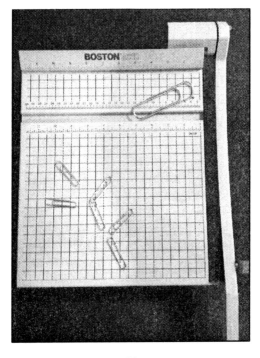

WRITING BIOGRAPHY

Bob tells me he is interested in writing a family history.

I realize we share yet another interest—writing.

"I have been in a writing group for 16 years," I tell him. "It began as a group of mothers with young children. We meet monthly and now the children we wrote about when they were toddlers are grown and a few are parents themselves, our children for instance."

"When do you do your writing?"

"Our monthly meetings are about three hours 7-10 PM. We choose a topic and we write for about 45 minutes. Then we read aloud what we have written. We are seven women who responded to a library bulletin board posting—an eclectic group—among us, a school nurse, a science teacher, a psychologist, and a librarian. What we originally had in common and still do, of course, is motherhood, but our writing goes in many unexpected directions. Inevitably, it is personal essays that spontaneously flow from our pens onto the pages of our journals—because we have 45 minutes to write, have come with no agenda and will read aloud. Of course discussion follows each reading. No criticism. No grammar correction. We say what we especially like about the piece—tone, dialogue, emotional detail—"You showed us so much about your relationship with your sister as you worked together in your kitchen; I could just imagine being there as I listened to your story."

"I like the idea of vulnerability with safety," Bob says. "You are fortunate to have the positive encouragement. Does it help with your writing done at home?"

"Some of us only write when we are together. Others are working on writing outside the group. I have written a short biography of my Dad. In our meetings, however, we focus only on the impromptu writing.

"I am interested in writing my family history, as it were," Bob tells me, "but I don't seem to get around to it. I would like to read what you wrote about your father. Has he seen it?"

"Yes, I think he felt embarrassed. Let's say he was 'moved' by what I wrote. My Dad is an emotionally tender man who is afraid to show it."

"I can identify with that," Bob replies slowly, momentarily lost in thought.

That was about all it took for me to make a bulletin board poster advertising a "Writing Biography" workshop. I reserved the Trustees' Room at the Concord Public Library for Tuesday afternoons and waited for responses. To those who called I explained the format— extemporaneous writing at the table for about 25 minutes, then reading aloud, with hope that we continue to write our family stories outside of the meeting time. We will meet every two weeks.

I told Bob about it.

"I'll give it a try, why yes!"

EVERYTHING I NEED TO KNOW I LEARNED IN WRITING GROUP

*Everything I need to know I learned in writing
group:*
How kitchen tables hold up lives
How pots of tea pour out words
*How pens moving fast across the page draw out
memories we didn't know we had*
*How filled journals multiply and spill into closets
and make us wonder what will become of them
and ourselves*
*How thoughts inked with trepidation become
lessons for ourselves and each other*
*How words leap off of private pages and take their
place in the world of connection*
*How our children, their lives caught forever on our
pages, become freer because our memories are
safe*
How we hold on to them to let them go
*How lives shared in writing are carried forward by
all of us, bearing witness to our strength*
*How all of our stories are, fundamentally, about
love*
*How taking pen to page is a journey with
meandering paths, straightaways, and unexpected
vistas*

Jane Wells
Concord, MA

In the Concord Library Trustees' Room we sit around a large glass-topped table used for 68 years in the White House in the 1800's during the administration of United States Presidents from Madison to Grant, (1809-1877.) Books written by Concord authors fill one wall of glass-fronted bookshelves radiating good vibes for aspiring writers.

We write for about 30 minutes. There is hesitancy to read aloud, but when the feedback is encouraging, shoulders relax and compassionate sincerity prevails.

Surprisingly, Bob is the most prolific writer of us all. In his soft voice, he reads aloud. The suggested topic one week is the word "Hands," another time simply the word "Should." Before you read the transcription of Bob's two pieces that follow, stop a moment and see what comes into your mind. "Hands." "Should." There are infinite directions you could go. What might you write?

Notice how impromptu writing brings to Bob's spontaneously written pieces the personality and thought processes of the writer.

HANDS
BY
BOB BUTMAN
SEPTEMBER 2000

One thing that is crucial about human hands is the thumb. Fingers too, of course, but the thumb is essential for good gripping. Humans are unique in this regard. The thumb allows us to use many tools that could not be used without a thumb. Try writing with fingers only.

I marvel at what I can do with my hands, I can hold the door key, a bottle of milk, a bag of groceries and a newspaper and juggle them all in a way that I can unlock the door.

I can do different things with each hand or they can work together to increase strength.

But while hands can do marvelous mechanical things, it is the way they express, or make visible perhaps, the personality of the owner that is miraculous.

Music, carving and painting demonstrate the mechanical skill, the personality and the brainpower of the owner. The laborer's hands we expect to be heavy and strong. The piano player's may have an octave-long finger span. Some of the difference is genetic, some is environmental.

So hands are major aids to communication and friendship.

Are hands more important than feet? With feet and no hands we would be leaf-eaters. With hands and no feet I can't imagine what we would be. We would have to learn to walk on our hands or roll through life. So survival may depend more on feet than hands, but our civilization requires hands (and of course our brains).

SHOULD
BY
BOB BUTMAN
SEPTEMBER 2000

I should call my 92-year-old sister. I should pay the bills. I should do the laundry. Or should I do something more appealing? Should is a nuisance.

But what if I say I should do the laundry and I do it? Then, obviously, that is what I want to do. People always do what they want to do. Or perhaps I should say they do what is least obnoxious of the options available. Of course, if you are securely tied to a railroad track (real or figurative) your options are severely limited. You may choose to laugh or cry but not much else.

Should must be a New England invention. It describes a reluctant adherence to duty but it doesn't change the notion that any particular thing that you do is what you want to do. When I say that I should call my sister, and I do it, I don't do it because I enjoy talking with her. She is forgetful (four repeats per call), she cannot hear, she has no news, and many complaints. I am saddened by her shortcomings. Each conversation brings her lack of options home to me. Her comfort zone is tiny. Her options are railroad slim.

Nevertheless, she is always pathetically grateful to hear from me and she tells me so every time I call. When I call I am somewhat discomforted for 15 minutes, but she feels better all day. If I do not discomfort myself for 15 minutes, I feel bad all day. So, I call.

Outside of class Bob does as he intended. He writes his family story. Not surprisingly, he writes enthusiastically about his early life, his seemingly effortless admission to MIT—the first of his family to attend college, his marriage to Oggy at aged 22, his military service, the birth of their three children, Marcia, John and Brad, his engineering career, the sailboats they sailed, their home in Concord and their house on Nantucket. But he stops abruptly. It ends with this line: "Life after Oggy's illness...."

It will be many more years of visits with Oggy, whose reservoirs of cognitive function slowly diminish but whose constitution supports her health. To supplement family visits Bob privately hires a woman who sits with Oggy, holds her hands and talks to her. Bob hopes that this, and members of the family showing up at random times during the day, will assure that Oggy is receiving the best care possible.

SERENDIPITY

Something wonderful evolves from our writing group when Bob shares with those around the table that his wife is an Alzheimer patient.

"I have done a lot of reading about the effect of music in folks with memory loss. The area of the brain where recognition of music supposedly resides seems to survive beyond speech. I have seen this with my wife who responds to my singing to her with movement and sometimes a smile or two. I wish there was more music included in the lives of the people living there."

Irene, one of the writers at the table is an accomplished pianist.

"Do they have a piano where your wife is living, Bob?"

"I believe so."

"I would be happy to come with you sometime and play familiar songs for the residents to sing along."

Bob is astonished at this offer and looks to me and back to Irene.

"I'd be happy to be part of that," I say.

"Let me talk with the management. That is a lovely offer. May I take your phone number and let you know?"

Expecting our visit, the staff gathers the residents in the center Atrium waiting around the edges of the room, the piano ready. Irene plays effortlessly, "I've Been Working on the Railroad," "Cruising Down the River on a Sunday Afternoon," and "A Bicycle Built for Two."— irresistible old melodies. Many join in or move in time with the rhythm. Oggy is attentive and smiling, swaying to the music. Bob is delighted. We return for a St. Patricks' Day party. Irene and I wear green sweaters; Bob sports an Irish green tie with his white shirt. We sing "When Irish Eyes are Smiling" and "Too-Ra-Loo-Ra-Loo-Ra." Bob and I waltz a little. They applaud and sing on..."It's an Irish Lullaby" and "Goodnight Irene." No question—music is enchanting!

Irene invites Bob and me to her home for lunch. Bob returns the invitation. He serves his homemade vegetable soup at his dining room table in Bermuda Green bowls he made downstairs in our pottery studio. Pineapple for dessert. We share family stories, encourage each other's writing and return to Oggy's nursing home to sing again.

Because of the Writing Biography Workshop, we, previously strangers to one another, probably know more about each other's family history than even our closest friends.

GEORGE

One day while Bob is out, I leave a long-necked, orange-beaked duck wearing a studious expression, a black top hat, a yellow t-shirt and a green-striped grosgrain belt on Bob's living room couch. A duck with a message.

"Hello BOB!" proclaims the note tucked in his belt. "My name is George. I'm here to keep an eye out, to let you know what goes on while you're away. For instance, someone came today, didn't even knock, came upstairs here and seemed to make herself at home. Just who does she think she is? I couldn't see from here but I heard her brewing a pot of coffee. You should be glad that I am an observant duck keeping watch while you're away."

Signed, "George."

To his surprise and puzzlement, when Bob comes home he finds a duck sitting on his couch. Orange duck feet, orange beak. "What's this?" He takes a closer look. This has to be from Jan!

He smiles, picks up the duck, opens the note and chuckles as he reads the sardonic "spying duck message," reporting what he's seen, assuming Bob will want to know. He rereads the

note then gets a piece of paper and writes one in
return:

"Dear George, I know she comes. She has a
key. It's fine with me. Don't be concerned."

Signed, "Bob."

He slips it under George's belt for me to find
tomorrow while he is out.

I move the duck up to the windowsill and
George reports on rain and sightings in the
neighborhood.

"Hi Bob, I think you'll want to know that she
was here again from 10:00–1:00, and where were
you? She brought her lunch, left something on
the counter there for you. I saw 11 chickadees
today and one annoying mockingbird. Signed,
"Your friend George."

When Bob returns to his empty house he
checks with George. Sure enough, another note,
this one complaining about a bird and a visit he
wished he hadn't missed.

So he writes back: "Dear George, I think the
mockingbird is quite remarkable, as is our guest.
Calm down, or I shall put you someplace with no
view, you fussy duck." Signed, "Bob."

I move George downstairs to the studio, dress
him in a purple shirt, sit him at Bob's pottery
wheel, and leave another note.

"Hey Bob, She was here again. She ate a lot of
pineapple. Without you! Made a mess with clay,
played the radio. Aren't you glad I'm keeping
watch?" Signed, "Your faithful messenger,
George."

Bob comes home but doesn't find George right
away. He's nowhere in the living room. Did he run
off with Jan? Was she here again today?

Later he finds George sitting on his chair at his pottery wheel, a smug expression on his duck face, a different shirt, a ribbon on his top hat and another note.

"Oh good, let's see what he complains about today."

I learn that Bob, who stays away from sugar, has, in fact, a favorite candy—chocolate covered cherries.

I buy Cella's individually foil-wrapped cherries and start leaving them surreptitiously here and there—on Bob's pottery wheel, in his refrigerator beside the pineapple, on the dashboard of his car, or next to his favorite chair. I imagine his surprise when he discovers one beside the table lamp. He leaves a note with "George."

"By any chance do you know the source of the chocolate-covered cherries? They are rekindling my sweet tooth."

When I find Bob's note in George's belt, I leave a candy beside George. No note.

REASONS TO GET UP IN THE MORNING

How many men living alone in their eighties decide to redecorate the living room?

"I've been looking at this furniture. Don't you think it needs a lift? I've brought home some fabric samples for new upholstery, also new drapes. Would you mind taking a look and give me your opinion?"

We are talking floor to ceiling lined drapes for two walls of windows and new upholstery for Bob's irreplaceable Danish teak couch and two chairs!

Bob shows me fabric very similar to the original upholstery—a light sandstone color with a woven texture.

"You've been shopping! These are lovely. This one in particular."

"Oh good, that's the one I like best. Thank you Jan. What about this for the drapes?

The fabric samples are a pale shade of ivory.

"Perfect." I say

"Done. Bravo!" says Bob.

The next day he returns the samples, someone comes to measure, and five weeks later the reupholstered furniture is delivered and the drapes installed. In the meantime Bob contracts for all the windows to be washed inside and out.

"I love this room," I tell him. "All these windows let the outside 'in'."

"Indeed, to me the sunlight is essential," he agrees,

"Now about the carpet. I'm tired of this one. Would you be willing to have a shopping trip? I can't fathom what would look right but I want a change."

So off we go to the carpet stores along Route 9 where Bob stands back as I swing through the rack of hanging carpets one-at-a-time like pages of a giant book. I look to Bob. He is shaking his head.

On to the next store where we repeat the exercise.

"Stop, go back one. What about that," Bob asks.

"Too dark," I say.

"Right you are."

"These are all contemporary. What about an oriental?" I suggest.

"Too busy, but I'll look."

Bob is right; they are mostly dark and very "busy" until we come to one with a light cream background and a subtle pattern in shades of soft golden brown.

"This one has the shades of the Teak wood and the sandy and cream color of the upholstery and the drapery fabric."

"I like it," Bob says, his eyes bright with surprise at the revelation. "It doesn't look like what I think of when I think 'Oriental carpet,' Sold!"

Without even consulting the price tag Bob motions to the clerk standing a watchfully respectable distance from us, hands him his credit card and asks for a delivery date.

Mission accomplished, back in the car I have a spur-of-the-moment idea.

"May I redo the bathroom," I ask.

"The bathroom?"

"Yes, the bathroom where you hang a fresh fingertip towel for me every day."

"By all means. Do anything you like. I'll write the checks."

I buy things in the light aqua color I know Bob likes—a shower curtain, ceramic hooks with matching shades of aqua and peach, a new white shower mat, a jazzy blue ceramic dish I made to replace the white plastic soap dish, two soft cotton rugs, also aqua and a set of towels to match. In our studio closet I find a small triangular shaped ceramic lamp Bob made and has already wired. I buy a white shade. It will be the perfect finishing touch glowing on the wooden bathroom shelf. Bob would never anticipate his lamp in the bathroom. From the wall in the hall I move a small oil painting of cherry-blossom-pink flowers in a gilded frame—a picture Bob bought when we went to the Lexington Arts and Crafts Holiday Sale.

I hope he hasn't forgotten the permission he gave me. We didn't discuss it after the carpet-shopping excursion. Too late now!

When Bob is out visiting Oggy and doing errands I nervously attack the bathroom, hoping he won't come home while I am balanced on the edge of the bathtub hooking up the shower curtain.

Success! I am innocently at my pottery wheel when he arrives home about 1PM.

"Lunch? Have you had lunch?" He asks.

"Not yet, I put mine in the fridge."

"Excellent, I will make myself a sandwich. Shall we eat on the patio?"

"Yes, I'll come up when I finish trimming this pot."

I hold by breath waiting for his discovery. I hear no exclamation. He probably hasn't seen it yet. But then, Bob is not one to "whoop."

Before I finish trimming I hear him coming down the stairs. When he stops across the room, I look up from my pottery wheel.

"Unbelievable," he says quietly, shaking his head, his long arms dangling, his palms facing forward. "You are a wonder."

OUTSIDE

Beside his front door Bob plants snapdragons lined up in rows like soldiers—an engineer's garden. Along the walk from the house to the garage he plants white and pink and purple petunias that spread and mingle enthusiastically in a jeweled carpet visible from the living room wall of windows. He mows his expansive lawn, trims his eucalyptus so it doesn't obscure the view from our studio window, feeds the peppy chickadees and goldfinches and the pair of cardinals outside his windows and cleans his own house, until I introduce him to Donna—a cleaning helper I have known for 22 years.

One cold fall day while Bob is out I brush aside the brown November oak leaves and plant a row of yellow tulip bulbs and a handful of daffodils to surprise him in the spring. When they push through the crinkly leaves six months later he is surprised and delighted but doesn't pretend to wonder how they got there.

Bob's favorite tree is the gingko. "One of these days I'm going to buy myself a gingko tree." He tells me.

"One of these days" comes along and Bob does just that.

"I've always loved the gingko. Wait till you see it change color in the fall."

He has it planted smack in the middle of his yard so he passes it as he leaves his driveway or walks to his mailbox at the end of King Lane. Its distinctively shaped green leaves turn a sun-soaked glowing school bus yellow against the blue sky in autumn.

In summer my husband and I spend time in Vermont. Without my company in Studio 55 Bob turns his interest in a new direction—the design of notecards picturing evergreens, leaves and flowers. It starts, of course, with a gingko leaf. It expands to include sprigs of pine, the burnt orange berries of the bittersweet, a small stem of the yew. Printed on ivory cardstock using his magnificent color printer (plus matching ivory envelopes), "RCButman Designs" is born. Family and friends receive a colorful assortment in packs of six at Christmas or for birthdays.

When the leaves begin to color in October, I bring Bob a handful of multicolored sugar maple leaves. The leaves are way too big for his notecards, but no worry, with his excellent printer Bob reduces the size and the "Fall Collection" is born. The following spring pink begonia blossoms and the flowers of Bob's 60-year-old kousa dogwood tree add pink and amber to his portfolio. He is 88 years old. His gingko tree is barely two.

"You cannot do

a kindness

too soon

because

you never know

how soon

will be

too late"

Ralph Waldo Emerson

(1803-1882)

UNEXPECTED GIFTS

In October Bob gives me two green and yellow gourds that look like long-necked geese, one tall, one small, set in sand in a dish he glazed Bermuda Green, facing each other in silent communication.

After a winter snowfall, while Bob is out, I build a snowman (no, a snow lady!) in his front yard. She has red and orange fabric flowers for her hair, dried hydrangea blossoms for big brown eyes and, of course a carrot nose and a scarf. She will surprise him when he gets home.

When my car is not in my driveway Bob leaves another pineapple on our doorstep. I cut it up and eat it until my tongue stings and I have to stop.

In spring he brings me a bouquet of pussy willows and in the fall, bittersweet.

I receive *Pottery Making* magazine in my mailbox. Could it be a promotion because I am a potter at the Emerson Umbrella? It has articles on how to trim a dish with an unusual base and rim. I bring it with me to our studio. Bob shows interest but claims no responsibility for the subscription. Days later I receive a postcard from *Pottery Making* magazine. "A subscription in your name is a gift from Bob." Which came first? I think I know. Bob concurrently subscribes to *Ceramics Monthly* and we compare and exchange monthly issues.

We go to holiday fairs together. At Harvard University's Radcliff Potters we admire the work of over 60 potters, gathering ideas for our work back in Studio 55 and at the Emerson Umbrella.

At a Christmas fair at Minuteman Technical High School we meander together admiring the artisans' work. Bob buys a walnut bowl turned to a satin smooth finish on a wood lathe and rubbed with teak oil. He talks with the gentleman who made the bowl, marveling at the revealed grain of the wood. I stop to admire jewelry made of twisted gold wire woven with thin colored ribbons and tiny beads.

"Pick one out Jan, I would like to give it to you for Christmas."

I choose a glittery pin and fasten it on the lapel of my green wool coat, not wanting to wait until Christmas. I tell Bob in the following weeks, "Everyone comments on this extraordinary pin."

"Yes Jan, it becomes you."

When Bob asks me what I would like for my 65th birthday I tell him "Your Jane Brody pancake party." And so it is.

Bob has breakfast parties. His specialty breaks his low sugar, fat free regimen in the very nicest way. Jane Brody's Multigrain Pancakes require 13 ingredients, two kinds of flour, buttermilk, and egg whites folded in at the end. No Aunt Jemima mix in a box. Bob has an electric griddle he brings to the table. No kitchen bustling required. Golden pancakes with his homemade beach plum jelly or Vermont Maple Syrup served on Bob plates, fruit in Bob bowls, and coffee in Bob mugs—all glazed Bermuda Green. A Happy Birthday breakfast for two.

Jane Brody's Multigrain Pancakes

Ingredients
    2/3 cup whole wheat flour
    1/3 cup white flour
    1/4 cup oats
    2 T flaxseed
    2 t granulated sugar
    1 t baking powder
    1/2 tsp baking soda
    1 cup buttermilk
    1/4 cup milk
    1 egg
    1 egg white (whisk until soft peaks form)
    1 T vegetable oil
    1/4 t vanilla extract
Directions
    Mix together all the dry ingredients
    Mix together all the wet ingredients
    Combine wet and dry, stirring briefly
    Fold in egg white

Number of Servings: 8

NIKO

Admittedly, Bob is not a "cat person" but Niko fascinates him.

My car is in the driveway. Our phone rings.

"Hello JAN, I'm in your driveway. I don't want to interrupt."

He knows I am home because my car is there; but he is not comfortable coming up to the glass door into our kitchen, unannounced.

"Oh, please come on in, you are never an interruption."

Niko, our Siamese cat, greets Bob at the door with her version of "Hello."

"Siamese can talk, you know. Niko's greeting is, for sure, more of a 'Hello' than a 'Meow.' "

Just inside the door, Bob bends and reaches down to scratch Niko's back with his long tentative fingers. Liking that, she circles his feet sniffing recognition.

"Hello Niko!" he says, a tad embarrassed to be talking to a cat, but equally glad she didn't beat a hasty retreat. Bob is someone familiar, he's been here before. Niko knows.

"Stay for lunch. I made seafood chowder. We can compare recipes." (Bob makes a fine chowder.) We bring two chairs from the deck and a small table to enjoy our lunch under the magnolia tree, which is in full bloom and just starting to drop white saucer-sized petals. "Delicious," Bob proclaims and smiles as a petal lands right on top of my head.

When we are out of town Bob volunteers to visit Niko, check that she has food, freshen up her water dish, hang around a while for company. He always tells us, "I think she was looking for you, not me."

But, that's Bob—self-effacing, humble pie for breakfast keeping him just a little somber lest someone discover how wonderful he is.

So potter that he is, Bob makes a bowl for Niko, a cat-sized bowl and for enticement he draws a mouse on the inside center so she will eat her food—all of it, and so... reveal the mouse! The bowl is the color of cream. The mouse, complete with whiskers and a pointy nose, is a shade of brown. "Not all mice are gray," Bob would defend if Niko, perhaps, objected to the color.

One Thanksgiving we cannot bring Niko with us to Pennsylvania. Our nephew Christopher is allergic to cats.

"Bob, would you consider having a long weekend visit with Niko. Instead of you visiting here, might she come to your house? We would bring her paraphernalia, her mouse bowl, of course, and her blue flowered cat house."

Bob looks skeptical and a little trapped.

"Oh Bob, think of the fun Niko would have figuring out your house, sitting on your lap. She loves attention as you can see."

"I have never envisioned a cat on my lap, Jan."

"It's OK, you can say 'No.' "

With trepidation, Bob agrees.

We deliver Niko and her food and gear.

We will never fully know what happened while we were miles away, but after that weekend Bob and Niko are fast friends.

Without prompting, Bob volunteers to "visit" Niko "any time she has to stay home... all alone."

All alone....Bob knows what all alone is like—a book or the TV his only company. Niko may be "only a cat," but in her way, she seems to understand and draws out Bob's affection with her own.

Niko is getting old—a teenaged cat. She develops a thyroid condition and becomes quite thin—like Bob. He comments on the fact. He worries about her, often asks me "How's Niko doing?"

Is she a mirror—her dwindling health a harbinger?

"Goodbye Niko," Bob says in July when Douglas and I leave for Vermont, taking Niko with us.

She is usually very lively. But not so much as summer hurries on. She doesn't want to eat. Her stamina is low. Before we go to bed, I hold her in my arms like a baby and sing to her. Although she has been listless all day, she lifts her head, looks up at me and gives a little yowl. "Stop singing," I read in her eyes. I don't know whether to laugh or cry. I lay her in her little blue flowered cat house and that night, as Douglas and I sleep a worried sleep, she dies

Bob's response? He finds it no surprise. She was 19—a sweet old cat, ladylike until the end. A cat, it seemed to him, with no regrets. A loving family left behind, left to grieve. Sad, yes, but unavoidable.

GRAVESTONE

Bob is busy with his recent project, unrelated to pottery or notecards. He is designing his and Oggy's gravestone.

Large sheets of heavy tracing paper are spread on the side kitchen table and Bob has sketched sailboats and gingko leaves beside and beneath their names: Olive Coolidge Butman and Robert Charles Butman.

"What do you think of this?" Bob asks me when we go upstairs for lunch.

Am I really consulting with Bob about the design of his gravestone?

I don't say what I involuntarily think, which is: for Oggy, whose life is so hopelessly miserable is it wishful thinking about a final release from her sad life? And for you, Bob, it's showing another side of your pragmatic nature since the gravestone will be for your grave as well as Oggy's.

Instead I say, "Oh, the gingko leaves! How did you draw them so perfectly? Did you trace one?"

"Right you are."

"But the sailboat," I say, "You drew this freehand, didn't you. It's perfect! Does it look like the boat you used to sail together? This is the jib sail, right? And that one little line under the boat, that's perfect because, of course, the bottom of the boat wouldn't show because it's under the water. You're brilliant! That one wavy line makes all the difference."

"Well, well, thank you for that feedback Jan! I think I am too close to the project to stand back."

That's for sure, I think. But with Oggy so sick for so long I do understand.

Bob lifts the top paper to reveal a different design, then slides that one aside to show me yet another.

"Lugubrious, I know," he says.

I am honored that he seeks my opinion and hope that by not overreacting to the implications and giving him my objective opinion, it will diffuse the undeniable.

"I think it's a heartbreaking project to do alone," I say "but it's beautiful that you can do this. I like the first one you showed me best—the one with your sailboat in the center at the bottom. I know from the stories you've told me that some of your happiest memories are of sailing together."

"Thank you Jan, that's very helpful; now let's put this aside and go sit outside in the beautiful sunshine. Would you care for some of my vegetable soup?"

VISITING OGGY

"Would you like to come with me sometime, see where I go, say hello to Oggy again?"

The last time I saw Oggy was several years ago at the Easter sing-along with Irene and Bob. Residents could stay at that facility as long as they were able to walk. Bob and his close-knit family had to find a higher level of care for Oggy, when walking, even with a walker, was no longer possible.

Oggy now lives in a nursing home 20 minutes from Bob's home. I am a passenger as he travels the familiar route.

"Oggy will probably be dozing but should waken. She will be in a wheelchair outside her room which she shares with another woman who is in no better shape, sad to say."

As Oggy's life slips gradually away, Bob's efforts to engage her attention or expect a response become increasingly frustrating. The realization that sometimes she does not recognize him does not stop Bob from his vigil.

The staff is always glad to see Bob coming. How could he not be a favorite? He is a faithful visitor. He plants flowers and tomato plants that he shares with the people who care for Oggy. As he does on the telephone, he uses each caregiver's name when he says "Hello."

We walk the corridor. I am familiar with nursing homes—the last stop on life's road for so many. The reality is never clearer than when passing the lineup of wheelchairs and someone reaches out to me and toothlessly says "Please take me home!"

Oggy is, indeed, asleep with her chin on her chest, like many of the people (almost all women) living here.

Bob bends to speak to her, his voice soft, his touch on her shoulder gentle.

Oggy raises her head, her eyes sleepy and unfocused. Her resemblance to the many photographs Bob has shown me is negligible. I feel a heaviness in my chest looking at the two of them. For me to be there seeing such vulnerability... it feels like an intrusion.

Bob straightens up and looks to me. Shrugs his shoulders. "This is Oggy."

I bite my lower lip, shake my head. To say "I'm sorry" is needless. I squat down. "Hello Oggy," I say putting my hand over hers. There is always a chance this seemingly one-way communication is silently acknowledged. Oggy pulls at her sweater, her brows furrowed.

I am reminded, so poignantly, of the divided life Bob lives, knowing how he soldiers on. My respect for him has never been greater. He handles what life has given him with steadfast, though unrewarded, faithfulness.

Several times Oggy has been rushed to the Emergency Room with grand mal seizures, high temperatures, and complicated infections. Bob has been told she is not expected to recover. Oggy's constitution and the marvels of medicine overcome these challenges. She is alive.

How long can this go on?

OGGY SILENTLY ASKS

Is not my fate
Worse than death?
Bent and incontinent
Slumped sideways
My daytime home
A wheelchair

Speech gone too
Only sounds remain
Lacking meaning
Calling for attention
What is it Oggy?

Wheel me to sunlight, please
To smell the outside air
Feel breeze in my hair
See the flowers
Hear birdsong

Your hands
Upon my shoulders
Melt my core
Do you know
Your touch
Is intimate?

I close my eyes
Your quiet singing
Revives memories
My head moves
In time

Like a metronome

All food
Tastes the same
Bland as porridge
Smooth
So I won't choke
Again

After sunset
The talking starts
Voices in my head
Jumbled
Coming closer

My bed
Not a safe haven
Rather
A silver-barred prison
Until morning

Why can't I die?
Just quietly
O God
Give me rest
No more elaborate plans
Why not
Tonight?

THE CALL

One weekend in late May I call Bob from Vermont to "check in."

"How is everything in Concord?"

"Oggy died yesterday. Her service will be next week."

"Oh Bob, I'm sorry. I'll be there."

"Thank you, Jan."

Bob's relief is palpable. His vigil is over. His grieving already lasted well over a decade. At Oggy's memorial service, held under a white tent in Bob's beautiful sun-kissed yard, he is surrounded by family and friends and neighbors of 50 years who buoy him with remembrances of Oggy—sailing days off Nantucket, skating on the Concord River, and skiing in the mountains. Bob is the gracious host of this celebration of Oggy's life and his demeanor shows no remorse.

Under the white tent sipping wine and eating catered canapés, Bob's son Brad introduces me to his friend.

"This is Jan... Dad and Jan do pottery together. Jan is Dad's... confidant. I think she knows him better than any of us."

OWLS

It starts with the calls in the night. "Whooo, who, who.... Whoooo, who, who." I listen for a while and notice slight inflections in the calls. It must be it a pair calling to one another, though the thought of an owl is a solitary image, wide-eyed head swiveling in panorama possibly looking for a late dinner.

Bob and I compare notes: "Did you hear an owl last night?"

"Why yes, did you?"

"Aren't they supposed to be good luck? I say.

"I believe the ones we hear are exactly that."

It becomes something we keep track of and mention from time to time.

At a yard sale I find a black metal cylindrical owl about a foot high (owl size) designed to be some sort of candleholder. I hang it in Bob's dogwood tree beside the garage and front walk, say nothing, wondering if he will see it. As more leaves come out following the white spring blossoms, the less noticeable it is. He doesn't see it apparently, and I forget all about it

However, without saying anything, Bob has taken the black owl from the tree and painted the eyes white, with green marble pupils, and put it right back. Now who's on "owl alert?"

The next time I hear an owl in the night I remember the hidden owl.

"I heard an owl last night, did you?"

Bob heard one too.

"Speaking of owls," I say. "Once-upon-a-time I saw one in your dogwood tree but I don't think you ever noticed him."

"In the dogwood? An owl? I doubt it."

"We better take a look," I say, eager to surprise him.

So, out we go, and right where I hung it, now almost completely obscured in the foliage, is the black metal owl with... Wait! The eyes!

"You found him and YOU gave him white eyes? You never said anything! You sneak! You just waited! How long ago did you do this?" Squeak, squeak, squawk I stammer on while Bob just stands there silent and smiling.

Weeks later Douglas and I are on a vacation trip. At a street market in Santa Fe a woman is selling small marble animal figurines, among them several two-inch high owls. I buy two—one white marble, one brown—symbolic souvenirs. I don't hide this owl; I just leave it on Bob's end table beside his chair where he sees it right away and where it stays.

It is the one thing I take from his house the morning after he dies. Now it stands on my kitchen windowsill beside mine. And the black metal owl with the green marble eyes? He is hanging in my magnolia tree almost obscured by the leaves that come out after the spring blossoms fall.

"A friend is

a person

with whom I may be sincere.

Before him

I may think aloud."

Ralph Waldo Emerson

(1803-1882)

"Friendship"

MORTALITY

You can't live in the same town for 60 years, read the obituaries and not wonder how long it will be until yours is there.

Bob calls it fretting. Not frequently, but often enough since Oggy's death, Bob talks with me about his fears—how they will compare with his fate. He visits friends in nursing homes who used to be his neighbors. He looks around his home at the staggering accumulation. He commits to getting rid of things. A box at a time. Out they go!

Bob is eighty-eight. Friends' names from his neighborhood appear in the obituaries. Bob puts on his one dark suit and attends funerals and memorial services. Of course he frets. He knows no one is exempt.

Regrets? Very few! He talks with his children, John, Marcia and Brad every day. Keeps the news straight about them and his grandchildren:

"Laura's planted rows of garlic.
Tim and Mike bought houses.
Dylan's gone to NYU.
Henry is at Bates.
John is writing books.

Marcia's in Roxbury.
Toby scanned a million of my slides.
Brad's gone out to Farley's farm
Nancy wants me to make a plate.
A platter, I should say."

"You forgot Jeremy," I tell him, "and if Nancy wants a platter, we better go downstairs and get busy."

But today Bob would rather sit and talk.

He tells me about his racing heart—atrial fibrillation. It comes and goes. He does extensive research, consults cardiologists to ask about all he has gleaned from numerous websites. His doctors prescribe medication. They suggest a risky procedure. Bob is wary. He has already had a cardiac ablation procedure gone awry.

He shows me his Body Data notebook where graphs chart his blood pressure and heartbeat irregularities. Records of health. Records of heart disease? He wonders if this will be his demise. Better, he admits than a stroke, or worse yet, dementia. Then there's cancer. But he recovered from that more than a dozen years ago.

"Every day I am thankful for my family and for this neighborhood," he says. "And for this house. I could never be happy in a north-facing house."

I know that sunlight is vital to Bob. He makes it a point to get his daily dose of Vitamin D every chance there is. He recently bought a chaise for the patio for just this reason. When I suggest a rocking chair might be nice, he succinctly rejects the suggestion.

"That just has the wrong association, thank you."

I think about the orientation of our house. In fact it faces north; but two skylights and the wall of windows in the open kitchen where we essentially "live" faces south and I am used to my eyes taking in the trees and gardens and the busy birdfeeders as an extension of the room. I remember Bob's compliment the first time he came to our house. "I like your house. Lots of sunlight."

I think about the apartment in the life care community where my parents live, (and since my Dad's death, my mother alone.) She has no south-facing windows. No sunlight streams in any of her windows. I mention this to Bob.

My mother is Bob's age. I have told him about her mild depression and her recent paranoia. She believes there is "a little man" who comes and takes a few of her cigarettes and sometimes hides things. She is convinced of this, although my brothers and I have tried to reason with her. She even claims to know who the mischievous "intruder" (she calls him "My Intruder") is. He is the groundskeeper she can see from her window. "The one who rides the mowing machine." Once or twice , she tells me, she has seen him in her room at night; but for some reason this doesn't upset her. "He's harmless." She assures me.

"I wonder," I say to Bob, "If the lack of sunlight could contribute to my mother's psychological problems."

"An interesting observation," Bob replies.

"Unlike you Bob, come to think of it, my mother never even goes outside. There seems to be no need or inclination. I gave her a wicker rocker with a flowered chintz cushion for her 85th birthday, 'So you can sit outside and read on the patio,' I told her. But when I visit her I see it is dusty and sprinkled with leaves, so she doesn't even get *indirect* sunlight."

"That's truly unfortunate," Bob says. No frills, no saccharine comments.

Bob met my mother. When she was visiting us in Concord he invited us to tea. I remember his succinct observation, (haven't I mentioned that Bob is not verbose) "Jan, you must take after your Dad."

I realize I shouldn't have gone down this path about my parents. When my father died five years ago, just before Christmas, Bob brought me seven stems of white orchids. They lasted 27 days, until January 15, my father's birthday, the day he would have turned 89.

"About my heart," Bob says, wiping his palms on his khaki trousers, "I don't know what I should do. What would you do?"

He wants my opinion. His life is at stake and he wants *my* advice.

He tells me he has read about the risks. He fears he will be an invalid, end up in a nursing home drooling in a wheelchair.

"I think you have already decided you don't want to take that chance," I say.

"And the alternative?" he asks.

"Keep on keeping on. Call me. I'll come over for lunch on the patio. Make another gorgeous Sine Wave vase."

Photo courtesy of Butman family

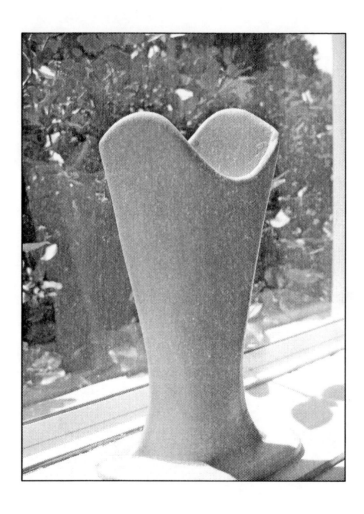

SINE WAVE VASE

Bob is tired of making cups and bowls. Without fanfare, he decides to make what he calls a Sine Wave Vase.

Sine wave: A curve representing periodic oscillations of constant amplitude as given by a sine function.

No, I do not understand that.

Leave it to Bob to calculate, measure, and draw a precise paper pattern using a wooden ruler, a French curve, a compass and a protractor, envisioning a vase with particular lines and dimensions.

He rolls the soft clay to a specified thickness using thin wooden sticks and a rolling pin. The rolling pin rides along the sticks compressing the clay to a uniform thickness.

Bob wants his vase to be 12 inches high. He must allow for shrinkage as the clay dries and is fired. No problem. Asking Google, he has found a chart to calculate shrinkage and determine final dimensions.

The wavy top edge dips on one side and rises on the other creating the sine wave. He also needs to make a base.

Ellipse: A regular oval shape, traced by a point moving in a plane so that the sum of its distances from two other points is constant.

Of course!

Bob's base is an ellipse, the two sides of the vase curving out to follow the line of the base, leaving a half-inch border all around.

Not only is this a marvelously engineered piece of artwork, but it cannot be assembled until the sides are just the right degree of dryness to stand vertically on the base and not collapse (which will happen if the clay is too soft), or crack (if it's too dry), yet be stable and still flexible.

No other potter would dream this up but Bob finds it truly satisfying.

The three pieces require meticulous seams. "No one needs a vase that leaks," he reminds me.

The seams hold securely. Bob waits patiently for several days as his vase, covered in loose plastic, dries slowly. Next the bisque firing in the kiln—another few days.

Now for glazing. After all his calculations, the final touch, glazing, makes Bob tense—surrendering control to unpredictable irreversible results.

He chooses, of course, Bermuda Green, checks the consistency (the specific gravity) of the glaze with a hydrometer and attempts the right application to assure a high glossy finish.

Together we load the kiln, set the dials, and throw the switches. Bob smiles through gritted teeth. Serendipity is not his style but now he must relinquish his treasure to the kiln.

A pyrometer measures the rising temperature. As he does every time he fires his kiln, Bob sets a timer, and checks the temperature every hour and records it on the graph he has drawn. While the liquefying glaze unites with the clay, he records time and temperature and connects the dots showing the rate of climb.

Check the pyrometer—twenty-three hundred degrees. Check the clock—nine hours. The glaze firing ends and the kiln switches off. Now, more waiting as the kiln cools down—12 hours more. Not until tomorrow may we raise the kiln lid, reveal the top shelf and marvel at the magic.

Bob waits for me to arrive the next morning before peeking.

"Let's do it."

He raises the lid. Voilà!

"Look at that Bermuda glaze, all shiny, just like you love it!" I purr.

Bob sighs, lifts his still warm vase, caressing it as he examines every seam and curve. Satisfied, he gives me his tight-lipped grin, satisfaction in his blue-green eyes.

"This Sine Wave Vase calls for tulips," I say.

The next morning Bob buys a bouquet of yellow tulips and sets the vase on his dining room table where the tulips open in the afternoon sunlight and close in the evening. The next pottery class day Bob brings his Bermuda Green vase of wide-open yellow tulips and sets it on the studio worktable. Now the tulips are dipping down, then swooping upward in a graceful ballet of compliment to the contours of Bob's vase. Of course, everyone comments. "How beautiful! What an elegant design!"

"Bob," someone asks, "How long did it take you to make this amazing vase?"

Bob just shakes his head. The question is unanswerable.

"The real marriage

of true minds

is for any two people

to possess

a sense of humor or irony

pitched in exactly the same key,

so that their joint glances

at any subject

cross

like interarching searchlights."

Edith Wharton

(1862-1937)

WINK

We are at an administrative pottery meeting, 15 potters around the studio worktable. The Emerson Umbrella Administrator is explaining policy. Attention is wavering. I look down the table and my eye catches Bob's. He winks—a silent message more intimate than a whisper. My tiny Mona Lisa smile is my reciprocation seen by someone else.

Some days later she says, "It's so nice Jan, you and your husband enjoy clay together."

My jaw drops.

"No Gail, Bob is not my husband."

Embarrassed, she apologizes.

"It's just... I thought... Seeing you together... It's nice actually."

JAN GIFFORD

SUNNY DAYS

At Rocky's Ace Hardware store I notice an umbrella table and four chairs on sale for only $99.00—perfect for Bob's patio, for our sunny day lunches. We go shopping, tie the heavy box to my roof rack, squeeze four nested chairs into the back seat, and with a couple of tools from his basement workshop assemble the table on Bob's patio. Perfect! Bob sits in the sun absorbing his requisite 20 minutes of Vitamin D. I sit in the shade supposedly avoiding wrinkles. Bob leans back, hands behind his head, sun on his face, and shakes his head.

"What?" I say.

"It doesn't get any better than this!" he sighs.

Another year of pottery. Another year of friendship.

For Bob's birthday on September 9th we go out for ice cream to Bedford Farms. We get double-dip cones of my favorite flavor—Chunky Chocolate Pudding—dark chunks of chocolate, pieces of fudge brownie and fudge sauce with some chocolate ice cream to hold it together. But not for long!

It is an unseasonably hot and sunny day. On the way to the car, our teetering cones begin to drip faster than we can lick. I laugh. Bob groans. "I haven't had an ice cream cone in years Jan, now I know why!" With sticky hands, we hurry back for dishes and spoons and many napkins. We laugh in the car, mopping chocolate ice cream off our clothes. Our sugar high lasts all afternoon.

SURPRISE PARTY

Most of the Emerson Umbrella potters are "part-time" potters and the variety of present or past careers makes us an eclectic group—among us a landscape architect, a state trooper, an art conservator, a pediatrician, a computer programmer, a veterinarian, an attorney, a nurse, and Bob, an engineer. Consequently, the topics of conversation are without limit. During open studio time there may be as many as ten of us working. Bob's schedule and mine often overlap. If we lose track of time, haven't brought lunch and get hungry, we take a short walk to the local supermarket's soup and salad bar to buy something to bring back and eat at the picnic table.

During class time the talk among potters doing hand building at the worktables and thrown work at the wheel can have many people talking at once. People who don't know Bob and see his two hearing aids sometimes assume he doesn't hear well because, fair enough, Bob seldom initiates a conversation. When the cross chatter escalates, Bob has a quiet trick. He dials down his hearing

127

aids and gets to work without the chatter. This is only discovered when someone stops to say something directly to Bob and sensing their presence rather than hearing their voice, he reaches to his ear with clay-covered fingers to "tune in." Outside, however, at the picnic table, without the sounds of background conversations, Bob's sharp wit surprises those who have already formed opinions. His popularity grows. He shares his engineering expertise by inventing measuring tools. Our teacher warns, "Make allowance for shrinkage, different clays shrink differently." A statement like that to an *engineer* requires clarification. Bob not only gets shrinkage rate numbers from the Internet, but he makes a rectangular rod from each clay body, marks and measures it, and fires it. By creating studio tools that show before and after firing sizes, Bob takes the guesswork out of shrinkage.

When Bob is turning 88 we decide to have a surprise birthday party—chocolate cake and champagne. Fellow potters are waiting in the large room upstairs near the gallery. Also Bob's daughter Marcia whose snow-white hair is thick and beautiful—unmistakably her father's daughter.

"I want you to see this amazing landscape picture made completely of quilted fabric," I tell Bob to lure him upstairs. At the top of the stairs, we turn right instead of left:, "Surprise!"

We have never before or since celebrated a potter's birthday. Bob is one of a kind, and enthusiastically liked by everyone who takes the time to get to know him. Happy Birthday, Bob!

"There is

nothing final

between

friends."

William Jennings Bryant

(1860-1925)

FRIENDS TO THE END

I inwardly quake—viscerally know what the title, *Friends to the End* implies when I unwrap my birthday gift from Bob; but I riffle through the book from the back—the same way I read a magazine, and smile at the 6x6 black and white photographs of animals with captions below.

I stop when I see a close-up of a bear—a particular favorite of mine. The bear is seated holding his toes (do bears have toes?). The words below the photograph put a smile on my face: "You could search the whole world looking for a friendship like ours, and you would only wear out a good pair of feet."

Bob nods when I read it aloud.

It isn't until another time that I look at the book's very <u>first</u> page. The photo is a close-up of a giraffe, who appears to be speaking? The caption below the picture, I now realize, is the reason Bob bought this book for my birthday gift: "It's not easy finding the words to talk about a friendship like ours."

So true, and you know, we never do talk about it, though we silently acknowledge it is an extraordinary relationship—age difference, gender difference, and the book title was spot on, *Friends to the End*. But stating it as such might burst the bubble. So carry on! If life is a carousel, we got the brass ring.

Are we ready for the end? Certainly not when it happens, although Bob talks about it. He is comfortable enough with me to admit his fears about the future. The question of whether he wants to be on a waiting list for Newbury Court— "a highly acclaimed residential campus in Concord to care for older adults as their needs change," the brochure promises.

Bob does *not* want to live at Newbury Court. He does *not* want to leave his sun-soaked living room or our jolly times in Studio 55. He does *not* want a small apartment instead of a home with a basement full of tools and a pottery studio coated with clay and a kitchen where he can concoct his simple suppers or elaborate pancake breakfast parties. He does *not* want to wear a coat and tie to dinner in a bustling formal dining room and be expected to converse with fellow residents. His hearing aids, good as they are, act up in a noisy environment. He would strain to listen. He would feign interest. He would *hate* the whole thing.

"Very depressing," he declares.

Bob's biggest predicament is his heart. It "misbehaves." It speeds up without apparent provocation. Occasionally we sit side-by-side on his living room couch and take turns taking our blood pressure with his digital cuff. Frankly, my blood pressure sometimes isn't great either and my heart skips beats. We commiserate, Particle 1 and Particle 2.

Bob researches his nemesis—atrial fibrillation—extensively. He sees his doctor. He takes medication. He consults a cardiologist. He consults another cardiologist. He drives himself to Emerson Hospital and calls me to say why he isn't at home in case I come by and find no note. I hurry to the Emergency Room, hold his hand as he explains Cardioversion—the procedure to get his heart rhythm out of overdrive and back to normal. This happens more than once. Bob's vigilance likely extends his life considerably.

So indeed, Bob and I are "friends to the end." The end is completely unexpected. He says cheerfully what he always says when I leave.

"Always a pleasure."

After dinner, apparently he lies down but he is uncomfortable. He calls his son John. His daughter-in-law Nancy answers.

"I feel a little off, I think I need some help."

Nancy calls Marcia and Toby, Brad and Farley.

His family hurries to his side. He sits up in bed, coughs, and dies.

My friend Helga tells me that when the neighborhood volunteer comes to her door to collect for the Heart Fund, she declines to contribute. "I think heart failure is the perfect way to go," she says. "Think of the alternatives, nothing any better!" If I could ask him, perhaps Bob would agree.

LAST GOOD-BYE

I am on the train coming home from Boston, passing Walden Pond where every autumn Bob and I walk the path together, all the way around—a good mile and a half. It's time!

"Today's the day," I say. "The leaves are peak, Let's do our Walden Pond walk."

Bob hesitates.

"I'm not feeling quite up to it today. My heart is misbehaving."

"Misbehaving? Like how?" I say, thinking last year may have been our last walk around Walden Pond.

Two days later Bob shows me a photograph he took when we were there last year—one of me wearing a bright yellow nylon jacket. Behind me, the water, the cloudless azure sky and the crimson leaves. I am smiling with the sun in my eyes.

Less than one week later he is gone. He dies at 89, a man with no regrets, completely keen of mind admiring red and yellow leaves from every window of his home. No nursing home. No hospital. No long-term care. No burden. No incapacity.

We spent that Thursday afternoon, October 29, together. I am sitting on Bob's living room floor with a newspaper spread out before me. I am carving a salad bowl with random grooves all over the sides. Bob keeps me company and serves tea and my favorite cream cheese brownies. A cup of English Breakfast tea, a pitcher of milk, a handy little bowl for the brownie, a small marbled bowl for the tea bag and as usual, a dinner-sized paper napkin.

He takes my picture unexpectedly. I look up and he takes another. It is the last picture on his digital camera.

Late that afternoon we load the kiln with our pottery, close the lid and switch the switches. Bob draws a graph to record the rate of climb measured by the pyrometer.

As usual, he sees me to the door.

"Always a pleasure, come again soon."

"I'll call before I come," I say.

"No need, likely I'll be here."

I walk the path from his door to my car parked in the driveway. Although we never mention it *per se*, at the end of the path I always stop and turn to wave. Bob stands at the open door and waves goodbye. Only this day when I turn he isn't there. I actually say right out loud "Humph, What gives? He always waves, maybe he went back to double-check the kiln." But I was disappointed. It was a first.

Certainly we had no idea it was our last "good-bye."

As I think about it I realize I can't say, "I remember our last good-bye." It didn't happen; and now that has meaning too.

Before dinner Bob likely took his customary walk along the streets of his beloved neighborhood, picked up his mail at the end of King Lane, passed his precious gingko tree, a nest of fallen gold leaves at its base, it's bare branches stark against the darkening October sky. He had no idea that it was his last walk.

BERMUDA GREEN – A LETTER TO BOB

Between your hands the wet clay spins. Your long fingers coax it round and smooth. It will become a little pitcher, one of a set. You will make three more, each a little larger than the last and you will glaze them with your favorite glaze—Bermuda Green.

Now they must wait a day or two, covered lightly with plastic until they are "leather hard"—firm, but cool to the touch—ready for trimming. On your pottery wheel, you will create a base of soft clay to hold each one upside down, centered and level, protecting its fragile rim. You will trim a curve and small foot with your sharp metal tools. Now for the tiny handle carefully connected at just the right angle. Add a decorative disk of clay? Yes, that looks good! Lastly, carve your initials on the bottom—an intertwined RB. Once the pitchers are completely dry, they will be bisque-fired in the kiln—the slow climb to 2000 degrees that will take 8-10 hours.

When it is time for the glaze, you have invented a tool to hold the pitcher so when it is submerged in the glaze your fingers will not leave marks. You are methodical. Your work never falls into the bucket of glaze. You don't drop it on the floor. You even built a wooden stand so the glazed pitcher sits above the tabletop and your tool can slide away. The other potters are in awe. You humbly continue, uncomfortable with admiration.

In your 11 years as an Emerson Umbrella potter, you make mugs, vases, lamps, plates and countless bowls. Seldom glazed brown, occasionally blue, you glaze most of your work Bermuda Green—"the shinier the better," you declare. You use it so exclusively, despite the fathomless choices, our potter friends affectionately call it "Bob Green."

The Thursday night you leave this world our pots are together bisque firing in your kiln. Alone in our studio I unload the warm pottery on Friday afternoon.

Your daughter Marcia asks me, "Jan, would you be willing to glaze Dad's pots before his memorial service on November 9? It would mean a lot to us to have them here—the last ones he made. Also, we wondered if you would like to say a few words at Dad's service. We *are* going to print a program, so think about it. We know how special you were to him."

"Yes, I will glaze your Dad's pots and I am honored to be asked to speak at his memorial service though I can't promise to do it without tears."

In the glaze room on the bucket of Bermuda Green there is a note:

"This glaze will be replaced."

I gasp in disbelief. Your favorite glaze replaced? Why? How could they? I am incensed! Is there enough to glaze your last pieces?. "Replaced?" The symbolism makes my heart skip.

My anger mixes with tears when I open the bucket and see the shallow puddle of the remaining Bermuda Green glaze.

I take a bowl from my shelf drop it in a plastic bag, swing it over my head and slam it to the floor. I am alone, crying in the cold studio.

I write a pleading note: "Please don't discard this glaze. I would like to have it. I will provide a container." I sign my name and leave two phone numbers.

Our studio manager, Caitlyn, leaves a note on my shelf. "The glaze *will* be replaced Jan, but you are welcome to have what is left, keep the bucket. Also, here is the recipe for Bermuda Green in case you want to make it yourself someday."

Two days later I tearfully tell the other studio potters and teachers about your death.

"Oh no! Bob? What happened?"

"His heart," I say, not sure if tears and sadness shared make things better or makes them worse.

"And Bermuda Green is going to be replaced."

"No!" they protest.

Voices are heard, replacement of Bermuda Green is cancelled. Caitlyn replenishes the glaze. The bucket is full. It remains a favorite of many, including Caitlyn; and I believe that in the minds of potters who knew you at the Umbrella studio, our Bermuda Green glaze is a reminder of you Bob.

NIGHTLIGHT

In the corner of the bedroom
On the hall table
On the outside porch
I wait
Till Twilight

Silent and inconspicuous
For a small fry
I perform mightily
Giving a glow
Here and there

Before and after
The home lights shine
I show the way
Illuminating the dark
Adequately

For the youngest
And the oldest
My reassurance of surroundings
Dispels confusion
Clarifies

For the toddler
Under the covers
My glow in the corner
Keeps the scary things away
Go to sleep

For the person
Up at night
The bathroom nightlight
Is just enough
Go back to bed

For the traveler
In unfamiliar rooms
I am the beacon
And I feel
Indispensable

Those who need me not
Teenagers
Behind closed doors
Claiming to know the way
Without assistance

They cast me away
Unplug me
Stick me in a drawer
Declaring
Their autonomy

Before alarm clocks ring
Or babies wake
My light goes out
I rest
Dark and unnoticed
Till Twilight

BOB LIGHT

On our entrance porch I keep the Bob Light on. It is a coppery brown pottery lamp Bob made for me. It has a caramel colored silk shade fringed with tiny glass crystals. The lamp is about the size of a bowling ball—a Massachusetts tenpins size, not a New Jersey bowling ball. It is not a nightlight. My Bob Light is a "day light." I turn it on in the morning and off before bedtime.

Bob had its twin. Same coppery brown color but with a green pyramid shade embroidered with amber beaded flowers. It was on a small table in our studio, right inside the door. Bob turned his lamp on at twilight and off when the sun came up.

Two miles apart they represented our friendship—brightening day and night—however each of us chose to think about it.

The bulbs burned out as light bulbs are inclined to do even though we bought the "long life" ones. I am a person of faith, not superstition, but the symbolism when the bulbs burned out spooked me, implying mortality.

Yet, the night Bob dies his lamp glows bright— and the next morning, and the next night.

Bob's daughter Marcia offers it to me. It was one of Bob's favorite possessions because of the unique green pyramid shade I bought, and because he made a matching lamp for me. Marcia knows this, which makes me even more grateful. Now Bob's lamp has a prominent place right inside <u>our</u> door and the one he made for me remains on our entrance porch. Together their light symbolizes a decade of memories.

PURPLE BOUNCY BALL IN THE SAWDUST

Year after year Bob's table saw created sawdust everywhere. A fine dusting coated the floor and no available surface avoided its amber touch, even though he invented a vacuum system with a motor and a hose to collect the sawdust in a box below, confining most of it.

Bob built the table and sawdust box with custom dimensions for height and width—his standing height (about six feet) and the width of the door. It has locking casters on the bottom which keep it firmly in place, but when the locks are released it is able to roll about, if need be, through the door, for instance.

But why? Bob wasn't going anywhere. The table saw was there to stay. But Bob is clever and insightful. He realized that eventually someone would need to move it out.

The privilege comes to Douglas.

Bob's family knows of their friendship and their projects.

"Doug, would you like anything from Dad's workshop?" Bob's daughter Marcia asks, as all his belongings go separate ways.

Douglas considers Bob's table saw a treasure steeped in the history of nearly 60 years of projects, many from the past that Bob told him all about, and several they did together. Bob could have written the biography, *What the Saw Saw* and Douglas would enjoy reading every word.

This gift is a weighty object but when most of Bob's possessions have been moved out, the day comes to bring the table saw from Bob's workshop to Douglas'. Sure enough, it slithers through the doorways, clunks over the threshold into the sunshine and rolls on its casters bumping along the flagstone walk. As Douglas tips it to push it up the ramps into his trailer, out from the sawdust box rolls a serendipitous talisman—something for me apparently—a purple bouncy ball with a smiley face! How did *that* get in there?

Might Bob have known? Nice touch!

I pick up the ball as it rolls to my feet, brush off the clinging sawdust and smile back at the face. I keep it—connect with the smile.

BLUE BUNNY

Bob's children continue the giant endeavor—clean out and sell the house and the accumulation of 57 years. "Jan, we're going to sell Dad's car, are you interested?"

I deliberate; have Bob's car be my car? Wouldn't it intensify memories, be just too much?

I can hear him say, "I love my car!" More enthusiasm than is usual for Bob. It took a lot for Bob to get jazzed up about something. But about his metallic blue VW Rabbit, he definitely was.

Finally, enough time passes and I rationalize—Bob would want me to say "yes." He would want me to enjoy his car, like he did. His family is waiting to hear my decision. So?

"Yes Marcia, I would like to buy Bob's car."

"Oh good Jan. I'm so happy, Dad would be very glad about this."

We meet and sign papers. I go to the Registry, get new plates, get new insurance and, once it's mine... I don't drive it.

I leave it in the driveway and drive the car I have been driving for seven years, my silver-grey ten-year-old VW Golf, (not that different from Bob's car). What am I waiting for, an epiphany?

I'm just not ready. How will it feel—driving his car every day?

My husband gives the car a nickname—"the Blue Bunny," but puts no pressure on me to start driving it.

Despite all my hesitation, I don't pick a special day for this transition. One Tuesday morning instead of taking my keys, I take Bob's keys to the Blue Bunny and drive it to The Emerson Umbrella—to the Tuesday morning class we used to take together. Will the other potters recognize Bob's car?

The car is a zippy delight. I love its bright metallic blue color. Amid the gray and black and tan giant SUV's in every parking lot, it is a little sapphire gem.

Bob's car, now mine, has a radio with an amazing feature considering my overactive startle reflex.

Bob knew how easily I startle. If he came quietly in the studio door while I was deeply in the "zone"—the clay spinning in my hands, he might just stand there watching me until I noticed him. I would eventually look up and be so startled to see him standing there that I would gasp, shriek and practically jump off my chair. He would shake his head in amusement and we would laugh.

So here's the special feature: Each time I start the car, the radio volume comes on very softly even if I left it cranked up loud listening to my favorite CD. Therefore...no startle! Furthermore, it raises the volume when I drive on the highway, compensating for road and tire noise, and then softens the volume when I exit to a slower road. These features feel like gentle acts of kindness especially for me. Nice Bunny. Does your car do that too?

EMPTY HANGERS

Nine empty hangers
Pants hangers
Without pants
Left on the table
Hollering

"We held the pants
Upside down
By the cuffs
Empty pockets
No belts

Disconsolate
In the dark
Paid no attention
Serving our purpose
Behind closed doors

We were ignored
Day after day
He wore the same pants
Clay stained khakis
Left on the chair

We held dress pants
Suit pants
Dark pants
Pants he didn't wear
But on occasion

JAN GIFFORD

Most occasions
Bob felt
Were overrated
Overdressed
Uncomfortable

In his khakis
And frayed turquoise flannel shirt
He was at ease
New balance sneakers
Woolen socks

Very little use
For ties
White shirts
Dress shoes
Pants on hangers

I think
They have run off together
The ties
The belts
Shirts hung carefully
And the pants

Wherever they went
Wherever he went
Apparently
No pants hangers
Are needed"

TELL ME – A QUESTION TO BOB

You can't tell me, can you? "How was your death?"

You can't say "What a way to go!" which many people say.

You can't tell me you were ready even though your clothes were sloshing in the washer, your dinner dishes in the kitchen sink, the pottery kiln heating up to 2000 degrees, and your latest porcelain bowl waiting for trimming on your clay-caked pottery wheel.

No, you were not ready. You were likely very surprised *but* (and this is a big *but*), in retrospect you would likely tell me you are thankful you were at home in your own bed surrounded by your family—grateful you didn't end up in a nursing home. We talked about that.

I hope it didn't hurt when your heart stopped beating, when your breath was gone and no more words could be said.

"Were you afraid—leaving here, going there?"

"Did you have flashbacks of your sailing days? Did you feel satisfied your life was full, never diminished or regretful?"

155

Tell me leaving wasn't hard at all because you had all a man could want—a long and excellent life, children and grandchildren and friends who loved you. I, for one.

I want to believe you were pleasantly surprised at solace and contentment beckoning you in an instant to something unimaginably wonderful.

Then I will tell you that many people miss you, miss seeing you walking in the neighborhood, working with clay at the Emerson Umbrella, miss hearing your warm familiar voice use their name on the telephone.

I will tell you I still have stories I know you would want to hear. We still have clay to share in Studio 55.

I will selfishly tell you that I can't rejoice. I miss you too much. But I would never wish a less comfortable ending to your fully engaged and active life. No one would.

"Tell me Bob, that in time I will miss you less, and finding traces of you everywhere, smile about the memories. Remind me that dying quickly surrounded by your family is everyone's unspoken prayer.

Tell me that eventually I will find myself agreeing with people who say:

'What a way to go!'"

SCATTERING ASHES

Here Bob lived at 55 King Lane for nearly sixty years, and here he died.

It is the following June, eight months later that his home is sold and his family and neighborhood friends come together to stand beside Bob's beloved gingko tree to scatter his ashes. I don't know what to expect.

Studio 55 is no more. The room is empty and clean. But in the enormous storage closet, Bob's pottery fills every shelf. His family wraps each piece with reverence, "Did he make this?" they marvel, asking me, knowing I will know.

"Yes, he made all of it."

In box after box they nestle his work in newspaper. I don't want to help with this.

So I go upstairs, walk around the rooms, to say a last good-bye, but I feel nothing. I sit on Bob's couch and hug the flowered pillow I bought him when he redecorated the living room. The hours we spent here, perhaps I'd feel his spirit lingering. But No! Only the roar of a lawnmower.

The Yard Man is mowing. Why now?

Neighbors and friends are gathering outside.

"Oh, he's running late," someone says. "Ask people to wait *inside*."

The Studio room fills with people waiting for the Yard Man to finish. There is still much more pottery to pack.

When the mower stops we file outside.

The freshly mown grass, green and even, is fragrant in the June sunshine. This beautiful day is a copy of the unseasonably warm November 9, the day of Bob's Memorial service here. We gather at Bob's gingko tree, now a burst of emerald green spring leaves.

Neighbors and family shuffle about waiting to share memories. Who will begin?

That's when the Trash Man arrives—more bad timing. He noisily chucks things into the back of his truck. We attempt indifference to the bang and clatter. Impossible, especially when he starts taking some of the family furniture. Apparently he thinks everything on the lawn "goes."

Breaking what is left of decorum, Marcia's husband Toby leaves the circle, talks with the Trash Man and the truck rumbles away.

A neighbor says, "Bob would find this funny."

I think she is wrong.

"Wrecking the reverence," he might say.

A neighbor shares a memory of Bob, then another. I am silent. My heart skips beats.

Bob's daughter Marcia gives some of us beach stones gathered at their Nantucket home. We spread them at the base of the gingko tree, still a sapling in its second spring. It will be moved to the Conantum Common Land, a remembrance of Bob—a founder of the Conantum neighborhood.

Now the ashes.

"Some of Dad's remains," Marcia says as she empties an inch of grey ash from a small zip-lock bag among the Nantucket stones. This does not feel, even remotely, like what once was Bob. No, I cannot make that connection—too great a leap. I just hope that when they move the gingko tree it thrives.

BEREAVEMENT

Our grandchildren have been visiting and they've gotten into the Tinker Toys again. They are less interested in sticking them together to make a unique structure than they are in hiding the round wooden pieces all over the house for me to discover when and where I least expect to: inside the tissue box in the powder room, in the butter compartment in the refrigerator, on top of the dirt in the philodendron on the kitchen window sill, which I find when I water the plant. It always makes me smile and imagine their delight as they scramble around when I'm not looking and find another wonderful hiding spot.

When I go to the toy closet to put back the "found" Tinker Toy pieces there is a blue plastic bucket full of red, yellow and blue fit–together plastic tubes. Without forethought, I pick it up and hurl it down the hall with all my might, then stand there crying. It is not about the mess I've made. but maybe about the fact that my "toys" have all been put away and there will be no more playtimes in Studio 55.

It must be one of those stages of grief, the anger one, in my case self-centered and short-lived. Am I allowed to be angry? Briefly perhaps, but please Jan, look at the big picture and get a hold of yourself. Now go pick up.

As for the acceptance stage, I am convinced that Bob left us far more than he took away. People who didn't know him very well might describe him as reticent but he held nothing back. A "full life" is an understatement to describe Bob's 89 years. His intelligence and vitality were genuine. His love and generosity to countless people unmatched. That is his legacy.

I am grateful to be called Bob's friend, to have shared his last decade. I am a better person because of our friendship and nothing will replace or erase the memories.

I remember what Bob said when Niko died: "She had a good long life, a lady to the end, no regrets, a loving family left behind, left to grieve. Sad, yes, but unavoidable."

"How lucky I am

To have something

That makes

Saying goodbye

So hard"

AA Milne

(1882-1956)

Winnie-the-Pooh

JAN GIFFORD

ACKNOWLEDGEMENTS

My thanks to Ruth Cross—my lifelong friend, my first reader and a thoughtful editor. Ruth has a long career as an Indexer. She appears in one of the chapters.

My daughter Lorell edited my manuscript and prepared it for publishing, arranging the pictures and the page setup in just the right way. Thank you Lorell.

My son Tyler asked me last summer, "What do you want to do this summer while Dad plays golf?" I said, "Finish my book about Bob." "Then, when Dad goes to play golf, you go to the College Library and do it!" I took his advice. Thank you Tyler.

My writing group is a 27-year-old treasure. Without their encouragement I would not have developed the confidence to write this book. Thank you Miriam, Molly, Nicki, Dee, Mandy and Jane (Jane's writing piece appears in the book.)

Jump Start Your Memoir is a 6-day workshop set in the beautiful Berkshire Mountains at the Kripalu Yoga Center. Led by the incomparable Nancy Aronie, 12 people sitting in a circle, write for about 40 minutes, and then read aloud in turn. First Nancy, then other writers in the circle share with the reader encouragement and insight. Three times a day for six days—total immersion. You live there. You don't go home to any distractions. Nancy is a loving leader who brings out the best in everyone—laughter, tears and good writing. Many thanks Nancy.

My husband Douglas had a wonderful friendship with Bob. His unquestioning understanding of my need to write this book as a tribute to Bob's life was a gift freely given. Thank you Douglas.

Bob's children read my manuscript. Considering it is the story of their parent's lives over ten years, and of their deaths, it is generous that they respect my writing this story of their Dad's friendship with me. Thank you Marcia, John and Brad.

To contact me:

Jangiffordalwaysapleasure@gmail.com

RB

Remember-Books

ALWAYS A PLEASURE